D1506328

SUCCESSFUL
INFORMATION
SYSTEM
IMPLEMENTATION

SUCCESSFUL INFORMATION SYSTEM IMPLEMENTATION

The Human Side

Second Edition

Jeffrey K. Pinto

and

Ido Millet

Project Management Institute

Library of Congress Cataloging-in-Publication Data

Pinto, Jeffrey, K.
    Successful information system implementation: the human side /
Jeffery K. Pinto and Ido Millet. – – 2nd ed.
      p.   cm.
    Includes bibliographical references.
    ISBN: 1-880410-66-4 (alk. paper)
    1. Information technology—Management.   2. Information resources
management. 3. Management information systems.   I. Millet, Ido,
1957– . II. Title.
HD30.2.P56 1999
658.4'038 – – dc21

           99–38110
           CIP

ISBN: 1-880410-66-4

Published by: Project Management Institute, Inc.
           Four Campus Boulevard
           Newtown Square, Pennsylvania 19073-3299 USA
           Phone: 610-356-4600 or Visit our website: www.pmi.org

10 9 8 7 6 5 4 3 2 1

Dedication

J. P.:

For my parents, Jack and Joyce. Better role models cannot be found.

I. M.:

For my parents, Amiram and Naomi. Best a tadpole could ever hope for.

Contents

Figures

Tables

Preface

THE BOOK REPRESENTS a second edition of the work, *Successful Information System Implementation: The Human Side*, published by the Project Management Institute in 1994. In the five years since it was first written, the field of information technology (IT) has continued to expand at a breathtaking pace. The types of technology best evidenced by computers and computer-aided systems have gotten faster, more reliable, cheaper, and ever more widely accepted in modern business practices. Unfortunately, our technical acumen continues to far outstrip our capacity for taking these IT breakthroughs and having them live up to their over-hyped billing in the workplace. Again and again, horror stories are told of companies investing in multimillion-dollar information systems only to have them become abandoned in midstream, irrelevant, or quickly outmoded. If this state was the exception rather than the rule in modern information system (IS) implementation, it might only be the subject of mirth, as organizations point to the expensive failures of the few who got in over their heads.

Unfortunately, no one is laughing. We are not laughing because no one is immune to these IS catastrophes. Information system project-failure rates continue to hover at 67 percent, an astounding figure when one considers that companies have spent enormous amounts of money in the past decade not only trying to install these systems, but also trying to understand what went wrong with previous failures. Lack of institutional learning condemns company after company to continue making the same mistakes—not just the mistakes of their competitors but replicating their own past mistakes! We seem unable to learn, unable to improve our project management skills, and hence sentenced to reinvent very costly and ineffective wheels.

Make no mistake; it is our conviction (and substantial evidence supports this view) that the failure of most IS implementation efforts represents a failure of project management. That is, most of the reasons these systems are not successfully implemented have less to do with their purely technical properties, and everything to do with their efficient management from a project perspective. Project perspective includes understanding scope and scheduling, goal setting, work breakdown, resource management, managing the *human side* of the installation, and understanding how to overcome the barriers to acceptance and use of the systems by their target audience.

This second edition introduces some familiar material as well as some new perspectives. One important change has been to move the focus of the discussion away from specific references to one form of IT—geographic information systems—and concentrate instead on addressing the wider family of all forms of management information systems (MIS). More and more organizations are moving to adopt these organizationwide information systems without adequately understanding how to best introduce them for maximum benefit to the widest possible audience. Expanding the focal point of the book is intended to attract a wider readership, who will perhaps find elements of their own problems or frustrations with their implementation efforts embedded in these pages.

The second important change is to introduce a co-author to this book, Dr. Ido Millet. Dr. Millet is a professor of MIS at Penn State-Erie and brings a wealth of practical experience and viewpoints to this second edition. As a former information system manager, he has experienced firsthand the problems with implementing IT projects in his organizations and offers a number of unique and invaluable contributions to the book. Together, it is our hope that *Successful Information System Implementation: The Human Side* provides a valuable guidebook to realizing the dream of new information technologies in our organizations through anticipating and offering solutions to many of the problems that have routinely derailed our installation projects in the past.

As with the first edition of this book, we would be remiss if we did not thank the behind-the-scene efforts of a number of individuals at the Project Management Institute (PMI®) who continue a truly professional commitment to the PMI Publishing division. Bobby Hensley has been an enthusiastic supporter of our work, for which we thank him. Ms. Toni Knott has been a great editor; her suggestions were always on target (knowing how to criticize the *right* way is a real gift). Jim Pennypacker, PMI Publishing Division's former publisher, is a good friend and has been an invaluable resource for PMI. His efforts are never more fully appreciated than by the authors, who see his impact on the publishing division and the stature of the Project Management Institute as a professional organization. Thanks again, Jim. Lastly, we would like to thank our families for their support in our efforts. For Jeff Pinto, his wife, Mary Beth, and children, Emily, AJ, and Joseph make everything else he accomplishes pale in comparison. For Ido Millet, his extended Friday-evening family, including his parents, Amiram and Naomi Millet, and Uncle Jake's family, though on the other side of the big pond, are a source of inspiration, energy, and insight.

The Problem with Information System Projects

Problems are the price of progress: don't bring me anything but trouble—good news weakens me.

Charles F. Kettering

The Evidence

Information systems (IS) continue to proliferate within our organizations at a breathtaking pace. Indeed, the advent of the much talked-about information superhighway establishes the context for the continued expansion of IS technology well into the twenty-first century. Something strange seems to be occurring on this road to success, however. Although there is no doubt that IS offer managers an unmatched degree of operational efficiency, it is also true that they present the casual observer with an intriguing conundrum: If systems are so advanced and offer the hope for such tremendous advantage, why are they usually used to only a fraction of their capacities? This question leads to a logical corollary: If companies are so committed to establishing organizationwide information technology (IT), why is the failure rate for new IS introduction so astoundingly high? The evidence is damning. Consider, for example, the following facts.

- A recent study of over three hundred large companies conducted by the consulting firm Peat Marwick found that software and/or hardware development projects fail at the rate of 65 percent. In other words, 65 percent of these companies reported projects that were grossly over budget, behind schedule, employed technologies that were nonperforming, or all of the above. Half the managers responding to the study indicated that this result was considered "normal."

- A study by the META Group found that "more than half of all IT projects become runaways—overshooting their budgets and timetables while failing to deliver fully on their goals."

- Applied Data Research surveys report that up to 75 percent of software projects are cancelled.

- The Standish Group offered an even more bleak picture of the current state of IT project implementation, stating that of approximately 175,000 projects costing more than $250 billion each year, 52.7 percent will overrun their initial cost estimates by 189 percent. Most of these projects are delivered with only 74 percent of the original functionality. The Standish Group concluded that the average success rate of business-critical application development projects is a miniscule 9 percent!

- A United States (U. S.) Army study of IT projects found that 47 percent were delivered but not used; 29 percent were paid for, but not delivered; 19 percent were abandoned or reworked; 3 percent were used with minor changes; and only 2 percent were used as delivered (*CIO* 1995, 5; *Infoworld* 1995, 62; Kapur 1998).

Of course, the picture is not universally bleak. (If that were the case, what, on balance, would be *any* organization's motivation to introduce IT?) Many organizations in the public and private sectors have successfully introduced IS technology into their operations and are highly satisfied with the results. For example, a large paper company in the state of Maine (U.S.) recently acquired geographic IT for land-resource management and automatic mapping of the three million acres of timberland it administers. The company has been highly pleased with the flexibility and efficiency that use of the system has added to its operations. In the public sector, Cumberland County, North Carolina, U.S., recently acquired a geographic information system (GIS) for use within four agencies of county government: transportation planning for public schools, tax-assessment mapping, community-assistance planning, and growth planning. Although the implementation effort has taken four years to complete, the results have again been very positive across the agencies targeted for use of the GIS. In fact, as part of a second-wave effort, new agencies are being earmarked for the system as expanding the GIS technology into other applications is considered.

On balance, the success stories of IS implementation have been impressive. However, they cannot overshadow the fact that at the other end of the spectrum, a disproportionately large number of other organizations have achieved nothing for their implementation efforts other than failure, lack of use or misuse of the system, and general frustration. The reasons underlying their failures are diverse and encompass a number of issues; however, it is our contention that the most frequently cited causes of implementation failure for these systems are behavioral and organizational in nature, rather than resulting from technical difficulties with the systems. Many of the IS in organizations that are currently underutilized or abandoned often arrive at this state not through technical faults with the systems as much as through inadequate implementation efforts on the part of the organization acquiring them. The examples are numerous.

- A large county in the Midwest was gearing up to begin using GIS technology after investing a large amount of time and money in benchmarking three competing systems and selecting the one it thought best fit company needs. Initial enthusiasm for the system was high, as the county supervisor was a powerful and vocal proponent. The problems began when it was decided that the GIS should be located within the offices of the county's computer and information department, staffed primarily by computer professionals. Worse, this department was almost ten miles distant from the rest of the county's offices, including those of the planning department, public works, tax assessment, and public safety—the four primary agencies expected to use the system.

    These agencies quickly discovered that in order to access the GIS, they were expected to schedule time well in advance to coordinate with one of the computer department's technicians. Further, little *real* effort was made to solicit their input into the uses for the system. Instead, the computer personnel determined the applications for the GIS and the order in which they would come online. In effect, the GIS became a bargaining chip in power struggles among the county agencies. Once the other agencies saw that the computer and information department intended to use the GIS in its own way, without seriously consulting with the most likely users, the agencies began withdrawing their support for the system and stopped using it altogether.

- Using funding supplied, in large part, by a federal grant, a computer researcher proceeded to establish a nationwide network of data-linked terminals for pharmacists. This system, complete with the most modern and comprehensive information available, was intended for use by pharmacists, to pull up relevant information on a variety of drugs: dosage levels, possible side effects, and generic alternatives. Since the system was installed some years ago, it has, in the words of its developer, "simply been gathering dust. The pharmacists are aware of what the system can do, they just don't use it." Follow-up interviews with a number of the pharmacists have demonstrated a general reluctance to use the computer. Intimidated by the new technology and unconvinced that the system offers anything radically different or better, they are more comfortable relying on traditional approaches to information gathering.

■ A small municipality in southeastern Massachusetts, U.S., spent over $750,000 on a state-of-the-art GIS. In proposing the acquisition of the GIS, the head of town development argued that this system was necessary for the township to be able to control the expected development and growth into the 1990s. When interviewed recently, the *new* head of development admitted that the system had never been used to its potential, in large part because the old head of development, its chief advocate, left the area to take a new job shortly after the system was purchased. Further, because the technology "looks" intimidating, only one individual in the office has attempted to operate the software. When he is busy with other duties or is on vacation, the GIS is not used.

These findings offer a bleak picture of IT projects in our organizations. Study after study points to our woeful inability to successfully implement the fruits of millions of dollars in investment, thousands of labor hours, and the priceless contribution of countless computer professionals. Computer-based systems have become the way of life in modern corporations. Unfortunately, the concomitant squandering of enormous financial and human resources in poorly implementing these systems has become a parallel legacy of our new information age. What went wrong? How did our ability to install and use these systems fail so spectacularly to keep pace with our ability to create them?

The Suspects

The answers to these questions are difficult and must be addressed on several levels. One point seems clear, however: Many of the organizations that have invested so heavily in these advanced technologies, and have so little to show for their outlay, may have only themselves to blame. In other words, many of the problems with bringing these systems up and online are not technical in nature but have to do with a fundamental failure of project management—the process by which the technologies were introduced to the company. The fault lies not with the techniques of project management, but rather with our inability to harness them systematically and exploit them in order to effectively introduce IT innovations within organizations. We have failed and continue to fail because we insist on viewing the *creation* of new IS as our ultimate goal rather than their *successful introduction*. The problem seems to reside in the manner in which these organizations have attempted to implement their systems: assuming that once the technical problems are worked out, acceptance and use is only a matter of time. How wrong they often find they are!

The problems compound; IS technological breakthroughs continue to advance at breathtaking speed. Companies, often following the lead of their technical staffs, become enthused with the possibilities that these new innovations portend, and push to acquire and adopt new IT. Unfortunately, about this time, the managers charged with the task of creating effective IS for their organizations often find that they run squarely into the brick wall of organizational reality—a wall most effectively summarized by the question of how to effectively and efficiently introduce these new technologies into their organizations so that the maximum number of people are able to make productive use of the system.

Difficulties with installation, however, are only half the problem. Even assuming we are able to "damn the torpedoes" and push doggedly ahead, finally installing our IS behind schedule and over budget, our troubles are nowhere near finished. We must still take into consideration system use and user satisfaction—that is, do we have confidence that the system is being operated to its fullest capacity, affecting and improving the performance of the maximum number of people? Unfortunately, to date, anecdotal evidence provides a mixed response to the question, how satisfied are you with your IS? While many users are highly satisfied and have made tremendous use of the various applications available through IS, others have not been as enthusiastic in their evaluations. Among the more frequently heard comments are statements such as:

■ "Nobody wants to take the time to learn the system."
■ "Because the system is in our department, no one else wants to use it."
■ "We never had any incentive to get it up and running, so there it sits."

These responses speak to one of the central problems that currently exists with regard to operating IS technology: the difficulties inherent in attempting to successfully implement these systems within organizations. Indeed, the term *implementation* involves more than simply installing an IS; it also refers to the degree to which the system is being used and the degree of satisfaction its users are achieving. When we look at the concept of IS implementation in this way, it is clear that companies face a complex and multifaceted problem when developing IT projects. They simply do not have the luxury of treating these projects as exclusively technical challenges. Rather, they must address all aspects of the technology and subsequent installation and system use if they are to truly capture the idea of IS project implementation.

Many of the conversations we have had with IS professionals demonstrate a general inability on their part to perceive technology adoption as a problem in the first place. Statements such as, "If the system works, companies will use it," demonstrate a certain level of naiveté regarding the true operation of most organizations, both public and private. Indeed, this attitude has been described by a colleague as illustrating the *Field of Dreams* mentality, named for a well-known scene from this film. While walking in a cornfield one evening, the character is presented with the vision of a baseball field while a voice whispers, "If you build it, he will come." It is my colleague's contention that many technical developers are possessed of the same conviction: If the technology is developed, potential users will flock to it.

There are a variety of reasons why implementation fails. But, the end results are inevitably the same: a significant loss to the organization both in terms of money spent acquiring the system and the opportunity costs due to loss of efficiency, down time for system hookup and training, and damage to employee morale when the newly heralded *wonder system* did not live up to its advance billing.

If this implementation problem is so pervasive, what can be done about alleviating the current situation? That question forms the basis for this book. The good news for frustrated IS managers is that there is currently a great deal of research in the field of IS implementation. Further, professional meetings and journals often provide important outlets for disseminating much of the results of *real-world* experiences in gaining successful IS adoption. Our intent in this text is to develop a *guidebook* to help IS managers understand new IS implementation. This book's focus is primarily behavioral; that is, it is our contention, borne out by a great deal of recent research and our own practical experiences, that many of the most frequently cited reasons for the failure of new system introduction are behavioral, or people oriented, rather than technical. Consequently, we will explore some of the well-known causes of new system introduction success and failure.

The preceding discussion highlights what will be a central thesis of this book: The success or failure of new information technologies is often directly related to the success or failure of an organization's project management of that innovation. Successfully supervising this introduction into the organization requires more of the IS manager than an in-depth knowledge of IT. Certainly, an IS manager's mastery of the technical aspects of these systems *is* very important to an organization's eventual effective and efficient use of IT. Equally important for new system success, however, is an understanding of some of the key organizational and behavioral dynamics that can determine whether the IS will be used effectively. In other words, we suggest that the quest for enhanced organizational productivity remains a *managerial* challenge every bit as much as it is a technical challenge. Thanks to a growing body of research and writing, technical mastery of IS has and will continue to get easier. As the technical expertise of many IS managers has grown, we are beginning to see the focus of their concern shifting to a concomitant set of managerial problems that must be addressed. While these managerial concerns (such as successfully implementing the systems and coordinating activities across departments) have always been in place, in an organization's rush to embrace and learn a new technology, it is understandable why they are initially given short shrift. However, the time to begin addressing these issues is at hand.

Toward a New Paradigm

Research in a variety of fields as diverse as the study of new product introduction, project management, and the implementation of management information systems has demonstrated the importance of managerial skills as a basis for system success. To illustrate, a study of project management conducted in the 1980s by Baker, Murphy and Fisher sought to determine which factors are most important to project success (Baker et al. 1988). Among the wide range of factors they considered were technical mastery of various project elements and behavioral and managerial factors such as leadership style, motivation, maintaining effective working relationships with other project stakeholders, and team building. Their research found that these behavioral factors were far more important for project success than the more technical details. This finding has been replicated in a number of other studies conducted on the implementation of new IS technologies (J.K. Pinto and Slevin 1987).

These findings have reinforced the importance of understanding the managerial roles and organizational dynamics needed to facilitate IS acceptance and effective use. In this chapter, we lay the initial groundwork for the discussion that will take place throughout the book, as we address some of the variety of managerial issues that confront organizations attempting to achieve the maximum effectiveness from their newly acquired IS. In order to develop a better understanding of the specific context for many of the examples we will employ, we will offer a framework that links that various components of successful project management with the unique aspects of IS. Our goal is to enable IS professionals to make explicit use of these principles in addressing the challenges of introducing IT in their organizations.

7

Structure of the Book: Processes and People

The chapter structure for the book follows a simple conceptualization of the component challenges facing IS managers in introducing new system projects. We contend that underlying the myriad issues that it is necessary to master, it is useful to adopt a framework that emphasizes the twin themes of process and people management as the foci for IS project implementation. *Process management* refers to an understanding of the context under which the project is being adopted, as well as the steps in selecting and organizing an IS project, the key components of *successful* implementation, the factors critical to project success, and so forth. *People management* recognizes that all project challenges are fundamentally based on managers' abilities to get maximum performance from their teams, understand the political and power relationships within their organization, and develop their leadership skills. Process excellence without an understanding of people issues is fruitless; command of the various people aspects without knowledge of process management is aimless. Consequently, the book's chapters are grouped under the following headings:

Process Management	People Management
Project selection and approval	The politics of implementation
The challenge of implementing systems	Project leadership
Understanding IS project success and failure	Project team building
Critical success factors in IS projects	Understanding project champions
Project planning and control systems	Cross-functional cooperation

Process management is vital in order to establish a context in which IS projects must be managed. Each of the chapters addresses an important element in IS process management. Let us first consider the issues to be discussed in process management.

Chapter 2 creates a theoretical backdrop for our discussion of IS implementation by examining streams of past research and their relevant findings. We are fortunate that there is a large body of previous research that has examined the implementation problem from a variety of perspectives. Among the important resources from which we are able to draw is research into the implementation of management science models, projects, and IS. We will use a historical approach to this analysis, following some of the early attempts to model the implementation problem, up to more modern conceptions of the implementation process.

One of the principal difficulties in dealing with the topic of how to implement new IS innovations is the fundamental lack of consensus as to what constitutes *successful* implementation. As Chapter 3 demonstrates, in the past, many people considered the acquisition of a new technology to be synonymous with its successful implementation. Later work has shown, however, that this judgment is far too simplistic. True implementation success consists of creating or acquiring a technology that not only *works*, but will also be used by organizational members and will result in enhanced work performance on the part of organizational units making use of the technology. Further, we will examine the idea of user satisfaction, showing that in many circumstances it is this satisfaction that is the best determinant of system implementation success, regardless of any *objective* assessments of model cost, schedule, or performance. As a result, we will argue that system-user satisfaction constitutes a more fully accurate representation of successful implementation than other individual measures.

Recent research in the implementation of new technological projects and innovations has led to the determination of a set of factors that can have a tremendous impact on the successful implementation of new technologies. The significant aspect of the majority of this research lies in the fact that the most important factors critical for implementation success tend to be behavioral, as opposed to technical, in nature, as well as managerial; that is, these factors are controllable by managers within the organization. In Chapter 4, we examine the results of a number of important studies in this area, discussing in detail the relevant findings and identifying the factors that have been shown to be particularly influential in creating an atmosphere that is conducive to system implementation success.

One characteristic that most successfully implemented innovations share in common is the meticulous nature of the adoption plan. It has been cogently stated, "Those who fail to plan are planning to fail." This dictum is never truer than in the case of attempting to implement a new system or program into an organization. Developing time frames, setting milestones, and determining work breakdown assignments for members of the implementation team are all vital elements in this process. Chapter 5 develops the idea of implementation planning, detailing some of the important planning duties in which managers must engage and explaining some of the more popular and useful tools for better controlling the implementation process, including work breakdown activities, PERT charts, Gantt charts, and so forth.

As we note, attending to the process details of IT implementation represents only half of the battle. Frequent consequences of inept people management of IS projects include quickly mounting problems, skyrocketing costs, and lagging schedules. One of the long recognized but rarely addressed factors that can play a vital role in implementation success is achieving an understanding of the impact of organizational politics in the adoption process. As part of our model of IS project management, Chapter 6 takes an in-depth, practical look at the political arena within most organizations, discussing the importance of stakeholder analysis for successful implementation. We will propose a model of organizational politics, and make suggestions on how best to navigate the political waters in getting new IS successfully implemented. In effect, it is our hope that this chapter offers IS managers some practical methods for controlling and influencing the political process, rather than being controlled by it.

One important duty of the manager charged with successfully implementing a new technology is engaging in project team development in order to create a cohesive and supportive climate for system adoption. Chapter 7 suggests some techniques for creating and maintaining a team that can strongly aid the manager in implementing a new IS. Managers are effectively setting the stage for the successful adoption of a new system by devoting sufficient time up-front to developing a cohesive supporting team. Indeed, this chapter highlights the importance of the IT project manager's role in successful IS project implementation, leading to the next chapter, devoted to a discussion of leadership activities in project management.

The concept of implementation team leadership is one that has generated a great deal of interest and research over the years. Unfortunately, much of what we know about this topic is theoretical and often contradictory. In Chapter 8, we outline some of the research conclusions regarding leadership behavior and propose an alternative model of implementation leadership, focusing on two important aspects of leadership behavior, delegation and participative decision-making. We suggest that the key to effective leadership behavior lies in adopting a flexible style, allowing the manager to respond to a variety of situations with alternative styles, as the circumstances warrant.

One of the most important but often unheralded actors in a successful IS adoption is the champion. A *champion*, as we explore in detail, often stakes his career on expediting the diffusion and acceptance of a new technology or innovation within the organization. Championing behavior has been found in a number of research studies to be closely tied to the eventual successful implementation of organizational innovations. Chapter 9 sheds light on the championing process, examining the roles and activities of implementation champions, and offering some prescriptions for organizations that would like to make better use of champions.

This book represents an attempt to develop and expound upon some of the most fundamental aspects of IS project implementation. In many ways, our desire to write this book arose from having witnessed far too many well-intentioned implementation efforts go awry. Unfortunately, a frequent side effect of these failed adoptions has been the strong inclination "to throw out the baby with the bath water." In other words, due to an organization's frustration with its less-than-smooth attempt or possibly outright failure in the adoption of a new IS, there is often a strong push to lay the blame for the failure on the characteristics of the system itself. The goal of this book is to begin to set the record straight, by developing, through a combination of theory and practical experience, some important tenets in successful IS implementation. Once we are better able to understand and begin to address the process and people challenges inherent to IS projects, we can start appreciating the full potential that awaits our use of IT. This book gets us moving down the right path.

2

Implementation Theory: What the Past Has Taught Us

What's past is prologue.

William Shakespeare

Numerous studies have addressed the adoption and diffusion of technological innovations in fields such as management information systems (MIS), project management, operations research, and management science. It is important to note that the terms, *diffusion* and *implementation*, are used interchangeably within this section. Historically, the concepts of diffusion and implementation were independently derived from different sources. Diffusion usually referred to the acceptance and use by some subset of the general population of scientific or technological innovations. The concept of implementation was derived from the acceptance within organizations of new technical processes or models. However, over the last several years, the two terms have come to engender the same idea. Therefore, for the purposes of this chapter, diffusion and implementation are both intended to refer to the process through which an innovation is communicated through certain channels over time among the members of a social system (Rogers 1983).

An understanding of the implementation process can aid in allowing those who could benefit from an innovation, such as a new technology, to begin accruing those benefits earlier. By identifying critical social factors and processes in the adoption, implementation, and utilization of a technology, we could better predict the decision-making responses of individuals, groups, and organizations and thereby accommodate or redirect these processes through prescriptive strategies. By identifying critical human and technical factors within classes of potential users, diffusion studies also have the potential for directing the design efforts of system developers to those system characteristics and improvements most valued by end users.

This chapter explores some of the important issues in the implementation of new information systems (IS) innovations, examining the historical roots of the implementation problem, some of the approaches to implementation that have been examined to date, and in particular, the distinction between content and process models of implementation. Through the development of a framework model, we show that the implementation process comprises a number of multifaceted issues, offering a variety of diverse but equally important criteria.

For the project manager concerned more with practical application than with theoretical background, this chapter could be read cursorily to consider some of the major theories of implementation that underlie later sections of this book. Another approach would be to skip this chapter entirely in a first reading, using it as a reference guide for examining some of the theoretical concepts more in-depth at a later point.

Implementation as Change: Early Models

Initially, the problem of implementation was discussed in the context of frequently ineffectual attempts on the parts of operations researchers and management scientists to generate enthusiasm for and use of a myriad of technical innovations intended for use by practicing managers. More recently, the problem of implementation has been represented as the frequent failure to create some degree of desired organizational change through the introduction of a new IS, program, or model. Indeed, implementation success has been defined in terms of changed behavior on the part of organizational members (Schultz, Ginzberg, and Lucas Jr. 1983). Implementation, in basic terms, is a new IS, program, or model that has been accepted by organizational personnel, the results of which change their decision-making processes.

Because of this perspective, in which implementation is predicated on the idea of fostering change, some of the earliest implementation models focused on the change phenomenon, viewing implementation as a dynamic process of gaining organizational acceptance. For example, consider two of the earliest and, in many ways, still most useful models of implementation: the Lewin/Schein Theory of Change (1952) and Kolb and Frohman's 1970 model.

Lewin and Schein argued that any form of organizational change must focus not on the technology, but on the organizational members who will be affected by that change. In this light, the technology, although important, becomes secondary to concerns about managing the attitudinal shifts by potential users of the new technology. Their theory suggests a three-stage process. Each of the stages—unfreezing, moving, and refreezing—is concerned with changes in the power relationships, which they termed "force fields," and the degree to which they lead to or prevent organizationwide resistance to the change. Unfreezing concerns any managed efforts or programs by top management to reduce organizational inertia. Typically, once members of an organization are put into a comfortable position with well-established procedures, they are loath to abandoning this comfort for change and potential hardship. Management first needs to establish willingness on the part of organizational members to consider the proposed changes. One of the best methods for creating a climate of cooperation is to demonstrate the efficacy of the new system and its benefits over old ways of doing things.

A recent example of this unfreezing process occurred within an organization that was considering the acquisition of an IS. Members of the planning department were generally unhappy with the possibility of moving to a computerized system, having to *learn computers*, and altering their well-established approaches. The manager behind the push for the IS arranged a field trip for members of his department to another local government agency a short distance away, and had this department's planning staff give a field demonstration of the new technology. Once his subordinates saw the IS in action and understood its capabilities and capacity for greater efficiency, they were very positive toward making the switch to the new technology.

Following unfreezing, Lewin and Schein suggested that the change be made, followed by a new freezing process, in order to cement the change in place. Freezing refers to any efforts that will confirm the new pattern of activities, through transferring *ownership* of the system to its users and making them responsible for successfully using and maintaining the IS.

Kolb and Frohman (1970) built upon the ideas of Lewin and Schein in that they also proposed a model of the change process, which focused on the important stages in the implementation. Their model is a bit more complex in that it offered a number of additional stages that had to be addressed in order for an implementation effort to be successful. For example, they more explicitly defined the nature of the client and consultant's roles in the change process, distinguishing between steps such as initial scouting and entry, as well as diagnosis and planning. Table 2.1 shows the stages in their model with definitions for each of the important phases. In general, their research built on and made more *actionable* the early work of Lewin and Schein, because it offered some specific steps that a manager in charge of the implementation process might take.

Where We Were and Where We Are

Literature in the area of system implementation, though significantly increasing in volume in recent years, remains largely unfocused. Many writers in the field have discussed implementation in a general sense, paying little regard to the type of implementation effort being performed, perhaps in the belief that there exists little or no real difference between various forms of organizational implementation (IS, projects, operations management/management science models, and so on). Early work on implementation tended to focus on the important *actors* in the implementation process, rather than on the *type* of implementation being considered. For example, one of the earliest studies discussed the need for communication and mutual understanding between the researcher or theoretician and the user, as a way to improve chances for implementation success (Churchman and Schainblatt 1965). Others also have argued for the need for formal feedback channels to encourage constant communication between researcher and user, supporting the belief that a key focus of implementation research should be on the organizational actors, as well (Schultz and Slevin 1975a).

The topic of implementation has also received a great deal of interest in public policy and agency literature. In fact, some of the earliest work on implementation, discussing the implementation problem from both theoretical and practical perspectives, used the public policy forum as a basis for analysis. The concept of implementation has also been viewed as a controlling and interacting variable, distinguishing between activities necessary for public policy enactment and those related to the implementation of previously developed policies. While much of the public policy work on implementation has largely remained unintegrated with the rest of the field of organizational research, this work has demonstrated the strong connection that implementation has with both public and private sector problems.

IMPLEMENTATION OF INFORMATION SYSTEMS

Information systems (IS) are a somewhat unique technological innovation in their current state of development. They require a combination of both centralized and decentralized processes for adoption by most classes of potential users. The classical implementation-conceptual model

Stage	Activities
Scouting	Client and consultant determine each other's needs and abilities; the department targeted for the new system is assessed.
Entry	The initial statement of the goals of the system. Steps are taken toward team building and mutual commitment and trust between the system's installers and the targeted department. Efforts are made to create a need for change.
Diagnosis	Data gathering to determine what specifically the client seeks. How can the geographical information system help them? What resources have been made available to implement the system?
Planning	Definition of specific targeted objectives, milestones, work (activity) breakdown, integrated planning, and resource allocation.
Action	Putting the system in place; making necessary modifications to the plan or system as events and contingencies dictate.
Evaluation	How well did we meet our objectives? Does the system do what it promised it would do?
Termination	Transfer *ownership* of the system to the targeted department; perhaps establish periodic follow-ups for downstream troubleshooting.

Table 2.1   Kolb and Frohman's Model of Implementation (1970)

presumes a centralized structure with a technological innovation originating from some expert source. Under this model, the innovation development process for a community of potential users begins with recognition of a need or problem, moves through research, development, and commercialization of the innovation, continues through implementation and adoption of the innovation by users, and ends with the consequences of the innovation (Rogers 1983). However, not all IS can be effectively classified under the same umbrella. Geographic information systems

(GIS), for example, are multipurpose tools offering advantages to different classes of users, which diffuse to or through them at different rates (e.g., utilities versus planning agencies versus scientists versus delivery services). Within each class, considerable adaptation or *reinvention* appears to occur before the operational characteristics and information-product capabilities are perceived to be beneficial across the class.

At the adopter level, decentralized implementation processes are often required to meet the differing information needs of each organization, along with the needs of groups and individuals within each organization. Decentralized communication and technology-transfer processes occur among and within similar organizations, which are all involved to varying degrees in tailoring the innovation to fit their circumstances. Although the implementation of IS hardware and software generally follows Kolb and Frohman's classical model, the implementation of data sources and data-handling methods appropriate to the class of potential users (e.g., types of data, quality and accuracy of data, means of collecting, forms of storage, forms of system-generated products) probably can be explained best by a decentralized implementation model. Thus, in studying the implementation of information technologies, researchers need to be able to identify the unique characteristics of both the system and the users to most effectively fashion a strategy for the IS' adoption (Rice and Rogers 1980).

INFORMATION SYSTEMS IMPLEMENTATION STUDIES

A great deal of recent literature in the IS field has focused on the process of implementation of technological innovations within public and private organizations. Conferences and agenda-setting groups have increasingly expanded the realm of IS research beyond the original development- and applications-centered descriptive studies to include investigations centered on understanding issues of IS acceptance and use.

The vast majority of IS implementation research consists of single-case studies in which practitioners and academic researchers report on the success or failure of their particular implementation efforts within a local government, planning agency, or some other end-user site. From these case examples, we draw conclusions that we presume to be generalizable to the larger population of similar users. For example, Levinsohn's experience with the introduction of a GIS led him to conclude that top management must be involved in major automation decisions (1989). More recently, Antenucci, et al. used case illustrations and examples to develop five types of implementation activities: concept, design, development, operation, and audit (1991). As Table 2.2 demonstrates, they were able to make some preliminary distinctions between successful and

Characteristics of Information Systems Projects		
Activity	**Success**	**Failure**
Planning	Rigorous	*Run and Gun*
Requirements	Focused	Diffused
Appraisal of Effort	Realistic	Unrealistic
Staffing	Dedicated, Motivated Continuity	Turnover
Funding	Adequate Finance Plan	Inadequate, Conjectural
Time Estimates	Thoughtful	Rushed or Prolonged
Expectations	Balanced	Exaggerated

From Antennucci et al. (1991)

Table 2.2   Elements of Information Systems Project Success and Failure

unsuccessful system introductions on the basis of a host of *managerial* issues, including planning, staffing, funding, and so forth.

Although it is expected that the eventual public and private investment in improved information-handling capabilities will be in the billions of dollars, few studies have attempted to correlate the usefulness of the technological innovation with adoption, use, and abandonment or to evaluate the efficacy of the technology in social terms.

Content and Process Models of Implementation

One of the serious problems with past research into the implementation of innovations has been the use of either a content or process model as the sole investigative heuristic. A content approach to implementation analysis focuses on determining those specific environmental, organizational, and interpersonal factors that can facilitate or inhibit the implementation process. Process approaches, on the other hand, strive to analyze the key steps or decisions in understanding how innovations are diffused. Although each method is useful, neither offers a complete picture. A thorough approach should identify both the key decision factors in adopting geographic information technologies and the processes by which the implementation occurs.

IMPLEMENTATION OF INFORMATION SYSTEMS: CONTENT MODELS

Under a content-model approach, data are typically collected from a limited number of case studies in an attempt to identify those implementation-model variables that are significant to the adoption process for the particular class of potential users being considered. Past implementation research suggests that in the IS environment we should be particularly cognizant of potential critical factors in the following areas (Croswell 1989; Huxhold 1991; Onsrud et al. 1989; Wellar 1988):

- visibility of benefits
- complexity in learning or using the innovation
- user's ability to try the innovation prior to commitment (trialability)
- compatibility with existing values, past experiences, and needs
- relative advantage of the innovation over the product, process, or idea superseded by it
- social norms
- existence of formal and informal communication channels
- appropriate balance between mass media and interpersonal communication channels
- extent and accessibility of vendors of an innovative technology
- opportunity for information sharing among colleagues
- presence or absence of champions, reinventors, and opinion leaders in an organization or the professional community
- how adoption decisions are made in the organization or within the peer group
- extent of reinvention necessary to adapt to local circumstances
- extent of consensus on methods and standards
- consequences of adopting innovations
- likelihood of unanticipated repercussions from adoption of an innovation
- memory of past failures
- presence of backups if something goes wrong.

This list is not exhaustive; for instance, one factor potentially affecting adoption is the *economic advantage provided by the innovation*. However, to date, in most technology adoption studies, the economic value of an innovation appears to play a relatively minor role in the decision to actually embrace the technology. Any institution considering investment in an innovation must first cross the threshold of having enough slack in its resources to make some initial investment in it. However, presuming the slack is available, factors other than immediate economic advantage typically are shown to be far more critical in the actual decision to adopt. Ad hoc observations of IS adoptions, for instance, suggest that numerous institutions and organizations are investing in IS capabilities, even though traditional cost/benefit analyses indicate that the investment will never pay for itself over the life of the software/hardware system being purchased. In other cases, although cost/benefit analysis strongly supports an investment in IS capabilities, the organization has been loath to incorporate the capability. The differences in the adoption decisions probably can be explained largely by isolating the critical implementation factors. What appears at first observation to be an irrational economic decision is converted to a rational decision when the critical factors in the implementation process are taken into account.

As the list demonstrates, typical implementation efforts often follow relatively similar patterns in terms of the types of factors that are most important. Further, as has been mentioned earlier in this chapter, it also becomes quickly apparent that many, if not most, of these factors are more *managerial* in nature, rather than technical. Implementation theory and research have long isolated the point that problems with the diffusion and adoption of new technologies are often based on human issues rather than on technical difficulties or concerns. This is not to suggest that a system does not need to be technically adequate in order to be accepted. However, as Schultz and Slevin's ideas of organizational validity and acceptance demonstrate, the battles for successful IS implementation are usually won or lost not in resolving all technical issues relative to the IS, but in appealing to and attempting to address organizational members' concerns (1975a).

As already mentioned, the problem with the content-model approach is that although it offers important information for managing a system's implementation, it is essentially a static representation of the implementation effort. In other words, content models do not mirror the importance of the *process* by which a new system is implemented. Most definitions of implementation have included as part of their descriptive phrases the process of organizational change or a change process. Consequently, implementation models need also to reflect the dynamic nature of new system diffusion. In other words, the content-model approach has value and provides insights, but should be used as only one of the components in a comprehensive implementation model.

IMPLEMENTATION OF INFORMATION SYSTEMS: PROCESS MODELS

Unlike content models of implementation, which are aimed toward identifying the factors that are the key determinants of innovation acceptance and use, process models are concerned with determining the key phases in the adoption process. One model suggests that there are two main sub-phases in the innovation process.

1. Initiation: The organization becomes aware of the innovation and decides to adopt it.

2. Implementation: An organization engages in the activities necessary to put the innovation into practice and incorporate it into existing and developing operations.

These terms, initiation and implementation, have been redefined by one set of researchers as the strategy and tactics of an implementation effort (Schultz, Slevin, and J. K. Pinto 1987; Slevin and J. K. Pinto 1987). Their argument suggests that one simplistic but effective way in which to view the implementation process is as a distinction between planning activities and action-oriented efforts. That is, planning activities (termed "strategy") are related to the early planning phase of the implementation process; they represent either the conceptualization of the new system implementation or its planning and control. A second set of factors (referred to as "tactics") is concerned with the actual process, or the action of the implementation, rather than its planning.

The essence of their argument is that conceptualizing system implementation as a two-stage process has further implications for system performance. Figure 2.1 shows the breakdown of strategy and tactics, by low or high score, depending upon the level to which these issues were addressed in the implementation process. For example, a high score on strategy would imply that the strategy was well developed and effective. This value could either be assessed in a subjective, or intuitive manner, or, more objectively, using some surrogate measures of implementation process (such as initial organizational member buy-in, schedule and budget adherence, and so forth). A manager could, for example, determine that the strategy was deficient, based on past experience with other, successfully implemented systems.

We can speculate on the likely outcomes for new system-implementation efforts, given the assessment or their strategic and tactical performance. Figure 2.1 illustrates the four possible combinations of evaluated performance of strategy and tactics. The terms High and Low imply strategic and tactical quality—that is, the effectiveness of operations performed under the two clusters.

Four types of errors may occur in the implementation process. The first two error types were originally developed in the context of the statistical testing of hypotheses. The last two error types have been suggested as the result of research on implementation. Type I errors occur when an action should have been taken and was not. Type II errors imply the taking of an action when none should have been taken. Type III error means taking the wrong action (solving the wrong problem); and Type IV errors imply taking action that solves the right problem, but the solution is not used by the organization (Schultz and Slevin 1975b). Each of these error types is more or less likely to occur depending upon the mix of strategy effectiveness and tactics effectiveness. An understanding of the interaction of strategy and tactics and their probable effect on project success and potential error type is an important aspect in understanding the implementation process.

High Strategy—High Tactics. Quadrant 1 in Figure 2.1 holds those systems that have been effective in carrying out both strategy and tactics during the implementation process. Not surprisingly, the majority of implementation efforts under this classification are successful.

Low Strategy—Low Tactics. The reciprocal of the first quadrant is in the third, where both strategic and tactical functions were inadequately performed. We would expect implementations falling in this quadrant to have a high likelihood of failure.

Low Strategy—High Tactics. Although the probable results of new system implementation are intuitively obvious in quadrants 1 and 3 in Figure 2.1, the results for efforts that fall in quadrants 2 and 4 are not. Quadrant 2 represents a situation in which initial strategy functions were insufficient, but subsequent tactical activities were highly effective. Some of the expected consequences for system implementations falling into this category would be an increased likelihood of Type II and Type III errors. Type II errors would occur in a situation in which initial strategy was ineffective, inaccurate, or poorly developed. However, in spite of initial planning inadequacies, goals and schedules were operationalized during the tactical stage of the implementation. The results of a Type II error could include implementing a poorly conceived or unnecessary system that has received no initial buy-in from potential users, and either may not be needed or will not be used.

Type III errors may also be a consequence of low strategy effectiveness and high tactical quality. Type III errors have been defined as solving the wrong problem or taking the wrong action. In this scenario, a need has been identified or a new system is desired, but, due to a badly performed strategic sequence, the wrong problem was isolated, and the subsequently implemented GIS has little value—it does not address the right target. Again, the tactics to develop and implement a new system

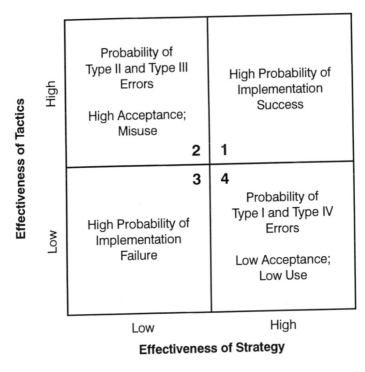

From Schultz, Slevin, and Pinto (1987)

Figure 2.1   The Strategy and Tactics of an Implementation Effort

were well conceived, but initial planning and problem recognition were poorly done. The result would be high acceptance of the system, as well as its general misuse, due to action being taken to implement a system when none may have been warranted.

High Strategy—Low Tactics. In Quadrant 4 of Figure 2.1 lie cases where strategy was effectively developed, but subsequent tactics were rated low or ineffective. One would expect implementation efforts classified in this quadrant to show a likelihood of Type I and Type IV errors (not taking an action when it has been determined that action is needed, or simply not using the new system). To illustrate, consider a situation in which strategic actions have been well performed and suggest the installation of a GIS. A Type I error would occur when little action is subsequently taken and the tactical activities are so inadequate that the new system is not implemented.

Finally, a Type IV error would occur following an effective strategy that has correctly identified the need for a GIS for the organization, but, after poor tactical operationalization, the system was not used for its

24

intended use by the clients within the organization. In other words, a Type IV error is the result of low client acceptance. As we have discussed, the reasons for lack of acceptance are numerous, but most often they revolve around a failure to match the system to the needs of the organization and its specific personnel.

Process models of innovation have been useful to identify the important steps in gaining acceptance and use of new innovations. However, process models by themselves are also afflicted with some difficulties (Srinivasan and Davis 1987). First, as mentioned earlier, most process approaches in the past have been highly qualitative in nature. Second, they do not attempt to determine who the key players within an organization are at each step in the adoption decision. Third, these models may vary or fluctuate to a significant degree, depending upon the type of innovation that the organization is trying to adopt. In other words, they may not be sufficiently generalizable. Fourth, it is often the case that the desire for *innovation* may exist within an organization at a particular *node*, whereas the overall organization is not particularly innovative. For example, certain nodes of an organization, such as engineering or software development, may seek to adopt an IS application, while the overall organization is reluctant to pursue computer IS innovations.

Conclusions

For managers attempting to better understand the management of IS within their organizations, a basic knowledge of organization theory and human behavior is essential. The goal of this chapter is to bring the reader up to date on the results of past IS implementation research. This is done in order to make the point that many, if not most, of the problems associated with managing the introduction and use of a new IS are *people* problems, rather than those associated with technical difficulties. Implementation theory and research have for years identified the most prevalent implementation problems (such as lack of acceptance and use) as occurring most often as the result of poor development of an organization's human assets. More importantly, content and process models of implementation have allowed us to better understand the activities within an IS manager's control that will allow her to improve the chances of system adoption and use. Consequently, any discussion of the process by which an IS is introduced and managed within an agency or organization must be predicated on developing a greater understanding of the organization as a social system.

3

Defining Implementation Success and Failure

Success depends on three things: who says it, what he says, how he says it; and of these things, what he says is the least important.

John Morley

The problem of attempting to determine information system implementation success is long lived. For the past twenty-five years, researchers have been making attempts to develop a useful, generally accepted, and comprehensive model of system success: one that takes into account all relevant aspects of information systems (IS) and their operations. This research, far from creating agreement and synthesis, has not achieved the sort of widespread recognition that had been sought. In fact, a casual glance at research into the implementation of IS in any of the major journals will quickly reveal that there are often as many different measures of system success as there are scientists studying the process. Unfortunately, the problems do not stop there. Another side effect of our failure to achieve consensus is that even when two researchers agree on the same general metric of implementation success (e.g., user satisfaction), they may be unable to agree on how or when that construct should be measured. What this phenomenon has created is a wide range of research studies, purportedly studying the same issues, and yet unable to agree on what comprises *success*.

27

This chapter is intended to create a framework for the study of implementation success by examining what the past has taught us, and how it can be incorporated into a better understanding of IS implementation. The good news is that underlying much of the verbiage associated with all these differing models and outlooks, there are some generalizable issues that can be brought forward to serve as a basis for establishing a more comprehensive and parsimonious model of successful IS implementation. Within this model, we see that a number of divergent research streams can actually converge, and that often our charges that different types of system implementation produce different measures of success may not, in fact, be true. Research done on implementation in other fields (e.g., management science) offers a great deal of utility, and has much to teach us in our approach to better understanding successful IS implementation.

There are several definitions of implementation success, many of which share some common underlying properties. Early definitions of implementation success were usually predicated simply on use or acceptance of the new innovation by its intended user (Lucas Jr. 1975; Mitroff 1975). The implementation process was generally seen as a bridge between system developer and user, which, once having been crossed, was regarded as successful.

Other definitions of implementation success have been more complex and thorough in their understanding of the nature of the factors relating to this success. Arnoff, delineating conditions for implementation success in operations research models, states that unless our models result in decision rules and/or procedures 1) which are implemented within the managerial decision-making process, 2) which really work, and, 3) which lead to cost effective benefits, our efforts are not successful (1971, 142).

A Model of Implementation Success

Schultz and Slevin offer an important contribution to the discussion of implementation success through supplementing these decision rules by demonstrating a behavioral perspective of implementation (1979). Their approach distinguishes among three conditions by which any implementation should be judged: technical validity, organizational validity, and organizational effectiveness. Technical validity and organizational validity are seen as necessary but not sufficient conditions for the implementation process to result in a positive change in organizational effectiveness.

---

1) Technical Validity

The assessment of whether or not the system's technology *works*—that is, it is a technically accurate and appropriate solution to the problem at hand.

2) Organizational Validity

Will the new system be accepted and used by its intended clients? Does the system alternative take into account organizational and behavioral considerations, such as the organization's culture, power and political realities, comfort level with computerization, and so forth?

3) Organizational Effectiveness

Does the new system influence the organization's ability to perform its work more effectively, make its decisions more accurately, or lead to profitability? This factor seeks to assess the *bottom-line* worth of the new information system, not only into terms of cost-benefit analysis, but also in relation to its impact on organizational operations.

Table 3.1   Schultz and Slevin's Model of Implementation Success (1979)

TECHNICAL VALIDITY

Technical validity is assessed in terms of the belief that the system to be implemented *works*; it is a correct and logical solution to the perceived problem. Obviously, should a new IS package be fraught with difficulties and other system bugs, it will not be used and, hence, will be regarded as a failure. Ashton-Tate Company lost a great deal of money and prestige in attempting to ship a new release of its flagship package, DBase IV, too early, before significant system problems had been debugged. Companies installing and attempting to implement the new database management system would have been unsuccessful due to the lack of technical validity in the package.

ORGANIZATIONAL VALIDITY

Organizational validity is assessed as a measure of the congruence between the organization and the system to be implemented. Most commonly, it is the belief that the IS is *correct* for its users, that it will be accepted and used by the organizational members for whom it is intended. Organizational validity states the obvious but critical notion that an IS is only as successful as it is accepted and used by the organization.

Organizational validity requires us to critically evaluate the current state of a company's culture. Is it accepting of new technologies? Does upper management take steps to reinforce new ideas and systems? If the answer to these questions is no, it is highly likely that no new IS is destined to succeed. A classic manifestation of organizational validity is the *not-invented-here* (NIH) syndrome held by many corporations. NIH refers to the parochial attitude that suggests that unless a product or idea is created in-house, it has no value. Simply put, the belief is that an externally derived idea will not be used by the company because it came from outside sources. Companies laboring under NIH frequently report serious difficulties with implementing new systems or other innovations because, while being technically correct, they will not be used by the client groups for whom they are intended.

ORGANIZATIONAL EFFECTIVENESS

The *bottom line* that any organization seeks through the development and adoption of a new system or other innovation is some measure of improvement, either in productivity, efficiency, or effectiveness. Early researchers recognized the importance of demonstrating some payoff from adopting a new IS. Based on the work of Schultz and Henry, it was further determined that new definitions of implementation success need to be based on the perception of implementation as a process of organizational change (1981). The basis for this view is that it is not sufficient to regard an implementation as successful merely because the intervention of a new system causes organizational personnel to change their decision-making processes in order to make use of the model. Successful implementation requires that the results of the system lead to improved decision-making, greater levels of efficiency, faster time to market, and so forth. As a consequence of this definition, a new IS that is in place but is not improving organizational effectiveness would not be considered successfully implemented.

New System Success—Modern Definitions

In spite of earlier literature that has offered a fairly comprehensive look at the implementation of management science and operations research, the measurement of success within the context of IS implementation has been somewhat underdeveloped. As recently as 1980, one of the leading researchers in the field of IS identified the search for the dependent variable (i.e., system implementation success) as an issue that required rapid resolution if the field of management information systems (MIS) was to position itself as an area in which viable research could be conducted. His point was that until such time as a generally agreed-upon definition of successful system implementation was established, our attempts at researching and disseminating information pertaining to systems implementation would be severely undercut by their failure to achieve a workable consensus. The importance of determining a suitable dependent measure for implementation success cannot be underestimated. A recent article states, "The evaluation of [information systems] practice, policies, and procedures requires an information system success measure against which various strategies can be tested. Without a well-defined dependent variable, much of information system research is purely speculative" (Keen 1980).

Since this call was sounded, over two hundred articles and books have been written on the topic of IS and the quest to determine exactly what constitutes a successful system. One of the surprising findings of the research is that it has been extremely difficult to build consensus on what constitutes a *successful* IS. As a recent article pointed out, of the hundreds of studies that have been conducted to date on IS implementation and use, there are almost as many individualized measures of success as there are research studies (DeLone and McLean 1992). Researchers and practitioners have rarely been able to agree on: 1) the important variables that should be considered when assessing success, and 2) how those variables should be measured, or, what comprises an accurate measure of any specific variable deemed to be important. As you can see, the problem now becomes even more complex. Not only is there wide disagreement over the appropriate success variables, but also even once they are employed by more than one researcher, there is often a widely divergent manner in which these constructs are measured.

The model proposed in this chapter makes use of elements of success that have been gleaned from a variety of sources—some from original work on management-science implementation, as proposed by Schultz and Slevin (1979), and other research that is more contemporary, dealing with success within the context of MIS. These measures of system success are intrinsically tied to the management of a wide range of organizational IS applications.

Information Systems Implementation Success: Toward a Comprehensive Model

Schultz and Slevin were correct in their early assessment of implementation success when they posited that any successful implementation effort is predicated on the technical efficacy of the system about to be introduced (1979). In other words, the technical viability and workability of the IS represents the first necessary but not sufficient condition for that system's successful adoption. Prospective users of any IS must first be confident that the technology they are considering does, in fact, work and accomplishes the tasks its advocates claim it can perform. This discussion is referring to the notion of IS quality. Some of the more obvious measures of system quality would include system response time, ease of online use (user friendliness), and reliability of the computerized system (absence of downtime). These measures represent some of the more common and accepted determinants of any IS' technical quality and should, rightfully, be addressed in assessing the chances for a successful introduction. Some technical characteristics are easily comparable across alternative IS, such as built-in features, expandability, system speed, and so on. Other aspects of system quality (i.e., user friendliness) may be more qualitative and difficult to rate, let alone compare from one IS alternative to another. Certainly, given the nervousness toward computerization felt by many members of organizations, attempting to develop and introduce a nonuser-friendly system may be a difficult and ultimately futile process.

A second measure of technical viability of the IS is the idea of information quality. The importance of information quality derives from the notion that any system is only as good as the information it delivers. In other words, rather than simply considering how *good* an IS is (system quality), a better representation of quality would examine the outcomes of the IS, the accuracy of the data. In addition to data accuracy, some of the most important metrics for assessing the information quality delivered by an IS are proposed data currency, turnaround time, completeness of the data produced, system flexibility, and ease of use among potential clients of the system. Additional elements of information quality are ease of interpretation, reliability, and convenience. These criteria exemplify ways in which we can rate the quality of the information generated by the IS, and, as in the case of system quality, provide a context for the willing acceptance and use of the system by its intended target departments.

The third aspect of IS success also relates to the earlier work of Schultz and Slevin's typology, as they identified their idea of organizational validity. Perhaps more than any other measure of the successful implementation of an IS is the importance of information use. Information use refers to the obvious point that information of any sort is only as powerful

---

A. System Traits

1) System Quality: The system adheres to satisfactory standards in terms of its operational characteristics.

2) Information Quality: The material provided by the system is reliable, accurate, timely, user friendly, concise, and unique.

B. Characteristics of Data Usage

3) Use: The material provided by the information system will be readily employed by the organization in fulfillment of its operations.

4) User Satisfaction: Clients making use of the system will be satisfied with the manner in which it influences their jobs, through the nature of the data provided.

C. Impact Assessment

5) Individual Impact: Members of the departments using the information system will be satisfied with how the system helps them perform their jobs, through positively impacting both efficiency and effectiveness.

6) Organizational Impact: The organization as a whole will perceive positive benefits from the information system, through making better decisions and/or receiving cost reductions in operations.

Table 3.2   A General Model of System Implementation Success

---

as it is accepted by organizational members and used in their decision-making processes. In other words, *useful* information implies *usable* information. Underscoring the difficulty of gaining system acceptance and information use is the problem of attempting to change employee behavior. During an interview conducted at a municipal government, one of the authors was shown the town planning office's IS, a PC-based version of a popular IS product. The system was quite literally gathering dust as the members of the department continued to make use of paper maps and old charts for zoning and public-works decisions. When the planner was asked why his subordinates were not performing these routine tasks with the town's IS, he replied that the PC's monitor had broken down over six months ago, but that it suited everyone just fine as they had never had much use for the IS! Here was a clear-cut case of the problem with acceptance and use of a system. So disinterested were the planners in the geographic-information-system-created data that they had seized on the excuse of a broken monitor as a basis for returning to their old practices.

Beyond the obvious point that a successfully implemented IS must be used is the more subtle issue of the different levels of use that may be found. For example, one study of IS implementation identified three different results of use: 1) management action, 2) creating or leading to organizational change (different ways of performing standard tasks), and, 3) recurring use of the system (Ginzberg 1978).

Another study expanded the levels of use in a manner that is particularly relevant to IS managers and users. In this research, four levels of use were explored: 1) for getting instructions, 2) for recording data (e.g., digitizing parcel maps), 3) for management and operational control, and, 4) for planning (Vanlommel and DeBrabander 1975).

It is clear that when *use* is broken down into its various components, it is insufficient for IS managers to state that their systems are being used. The logical follow-up to such a statement is to ask how the system is being used. In other words, is the system being used to its fullest capabilities, or is the organization content to use the IS to perform a few minor functions without really testing its capacity?

One of the most common (but difficult to assess) measures of IS success is user satisfaction. It is important to distinguish between system use and user satisfaction with the system. In many cases, a system may be used to a marginal degree without generating much satisfaction on the part of its users, particularly if there are no viable alternatives. In fact, a rule of thumb often suggests that underutilized systems exist because they do not elicit much satisfaction from their users. User satisfaction, on the other hand, is an extremely relevant measure of implementation success in that it refers to the level of acceptance and positive feelings toward the IS. It is important to note that user satisfaction has to be assessed after the fact. The users must be in a position to evaluate the data generated, the ease with which they were able to create this data—whether or not the system meets its advertised goals—and so forth. In spite of these examples of issues that can influence user satisfaction, the concept itself remains very difficult to accurately assess. In effect, user satisfaction asks managers to get inside the heads of the users to see exactly what it is about the system that appeals to them. Even then, a second difficulty relates to determining relative levels of satisfaction. Does satisfaction mean the same thing to different users?

At this point, we need to consider other difficulties in employing user satisfaction as a measure of implementation success. In particular, two additional questions arise:

1. Whose satisfaction should be measured?

2. How do we separate individuals' general attitudes toward computers from their satisfaction with this specific technology?

In other words, many groups or individuals within the organization could potentially make use of IS technology. An obvious problem arises when there is a wide discrepancy in terms of their relative levels of satisfaction with the IS. Why is it working well for some departments and not for others? This question seeks to determine the reasons that the system's introduction is being handled better in some areas of the organization than in others. Another difficulty with measuring satisfaction has to do with the potential for differential satisfaction at various organizational levels. Top management may be extremely pleased with the IS while the lower, operational levels are only minimally applying the technology and doing everything possible to avoid using it. Obviously, the *true* measure of user satisfaction in this case rests with the lower-level managers and staff who are ostensibly using a system with which they are quite dissatisfied.

The second concern with regard to user satisfaction is one that has been articulated well in the IS literature. This problem has to do with the obvious link between user satisfaction and the user's overall attitude (positive or negative) regarding the use of computers. It is no secret that many individuals in most public and private organizations manifest a great deal of anxiety when confronted with computers. This *computer anxiety* has been the cause of many voluntary withdrawals from companies, as departments are seeking to computerize without spending adequate time retraining employees. On the other hand, newer generations of American workers, growing up accustomed to the presence and utility of computers, generally possess a much more positive attitude toward their capabilities. This positive attitude is often reflective of their general level of satisfaction with newly introduced computer systems. The point that needs to be stressed for managers is that prior to the attempted implementation of an IS, it is extremely important that adequate time be spent in assessing the general attitudes regarding computers on the part of impacted departments. If the perception is that these attitudes are not as positive as they should be, a program in computer training for personnel prior to system introduction is not only useful but also often absolutely necessary.

Organizations usually do not adopt new often-expensive technologies simply for their own sakes. Rather, as a bottom line, they seek some form of return on their investments. In other words, what is the potential payoff for using the IS? This point underlines the final two assessments of implementation success: individual impact and organizational impact. Individual impact refers to "my expectation that through use of the new IS (through the effect of enhanced information availability), I will derive positive benefits"; that is, "I believe that using IS technology in my operations will make me a better employee, subordinate, governmental agent, or manager." In determining the individual impact of an IS, there are a number of points that managers need to bear in mind. For example, *impact* could refer to an improvement in the subordinate's performance; perhaps the IS allows the employee to make better, more complete, or more accurate decisions. However, impact can also be assessed in other ways. For instance, as has been noted: impact could be an indication that an IS has given the user a better understanding of the decision context, improved his decision-making productivity, produced a change in user activity, or changed the decision-maker's perception of the importance or usefulness of the IS (DeLone and McLean 1992, 69).

One can see that, defined in this manner, the concept of user impact is truly multifaceted. It is comprised of not just an assessment that the IS makes better (more efficient and effective) employees, but that it also creates a more professional, well-reasoned workforce—one that is capable of using the IS technology as a stepping stone to knowledge enhancement. Put in this light, IS can have the power to teach, as well as nurture, better informed workers through allowing these employees to understand and grow with the system and its capabilities. As a result, when assessing individual impact, the manager may be at a disadvantage in knowing at what point to make that determination. When will individual impact be realized to a degree that is noticeable and attributable to the influence of the IS? We will discuss this issue of timing in impact assessment in more detail later in this chapter.

Another aspect of bottom-line assessment of an IS' success lies in its relationship to organizational impact. As Schultz and Slevin have argued, any measure of system implementation success has to take into account some level of expected resultant increase in performance through adopting the technology (1979). Top management must understandably seek some payoff for its investment of time, money, and human resources in adopting IS technology. Certainly, within the public sector, it is reasonable to expect municipal authorities to ask some tough questions regarding the expected gains from use of an IS prior to sanctioning its purchase.

Unfortunately, the determination of organizational impact through adoption of IS technology may be highly uncertain and has been the source of enormous debate within the IS field for years. In fact, many researchers are entirely uncomfortable with the idea that an IS must generate some concrete payoff to its organization, preferring to stress other ways in which the system has impacted the organization. For example, they argue, if the system has caused an organization's employees to apply computerized technologies to new problem areas that had previously been ignored or thought inappropriate for its use, the system has demonstrated positive returns. Further, cost-reduction figures may be difficult to generate as they are often measured in terms of time saved through using the IS over other, traditional work methods.

Assessing a system's impact on organizational effectiveness may further be problematic in that it is often difficult to single out the true effects of the IS from other biasing or historically moderating effects. In other words, the organization is not simply standing still while a new IS is brought up and running. Other external events are affecting the organization and its ability to function effectively. Consequently, it may be difficult to parse out the true impact of an IS from other activities and events that are influencing the operations of the organization. These and similar issues have combined to make any accurate assessment of organizational impact difficult at best.

The Assessment of Success Over Time

One of the points that has been repeatedly stressed in this chapter is the necessity of developing an adequate program in terms of knowing when to determine system implementation success. As has been mentioned, there are definite benefits involved in waiting until after the system has been put in place and is being used by its intended clients before assessing the success and impact of the system. On the other hand, we must be careful not to wait so long to determine system impact and implementation success that the possibility exists of other organizational or external environmental factors influencing the organization to the point where we are unable to determine the relative impact of the IS on operations.

Figure 3.2 illustrates the difficulty faced by the implementation team and manager, showing a simple time line, demonstrating the point at which various aspects of implementation success can be evaluated. At the earlier stages in the implementation process, the typical assessments of success tend to revolve around internal organizational factors, such as adherence to budget and schedule, performance capabilities, project team cooperation and productivity, and project team/parent organization relationships. The loop in the system represents the instance or instances when periodic assessments of these internal criteria are made. If major discrepancies exist in any of these criteria, the implementation effort is

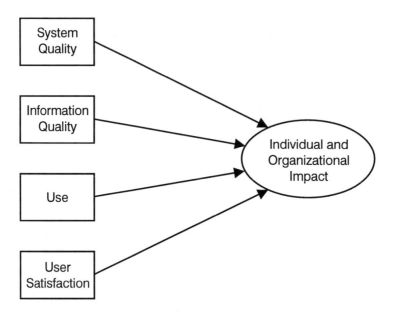

Figure 3.1   Modeling the Determinants of System Implementation Success

quite often extended, reconsidered, rebudgeted, or, sometimes, even scrapped. About midpoint in the time line is the installation point. At this stage, a number of projections regarding the system's success are being made. The IS is examined in terms of its technical capabilities (Have pilot project results been satisfactory?), including information and system quality. While performance capabilities will become and remain very important, some other traditional measures of internal success become less so. For example, by this point, acquisition and installation schedules have been completed; the scheduling that remains pertains largely to training and bringing additional software features online. Further, the majority of the budget has already been expended at this stage. On the other hand, the use and impact factors are continuing to be of greater importance now that the system has been installed, handed over to its prospective users, and is up and running.

As the time line in Figure 3.2 continues to the right, it becomes pro-gressively more wavy, symbolizing the increasing difficulty in accurately measuring system implementation success based on concepts such as *organizational impact* and *perceived value of the system*. Because the system now resides with its users, their departmental activities and current states

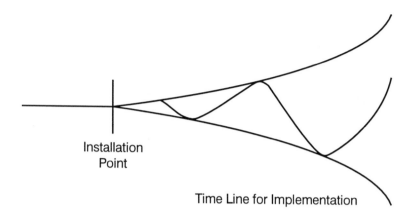

Installation
Point

Time Line for Implementation

Figure 3.2   Assessment of System Success Over Time

of operations will continually have an impact on the system. As a result, sometimes the IS will initially be hailed as an important breakthrough, but down the road it suddenly becomes obsolete. On the other hand, some IS, which were regarded early on as a waste of money or worse, will now be viewed as being very important to the organization and will be considered successes.

Figure 3.2 suggests that while periodic assessments of the current state of the implemented system are important, an accurate determination of the ultimate success or failure of a project is equally important. The difficulty lies in attempting to find a suitable reference point at which time the system has been transferred to the clients, is up and running, and is making some initial impact on organizational effectiveness. One of the important benefits of using such a *post-installation* system assessment point is that it drives home the idea to many implementation team leaders that their duties to the IS do not end when the system is acquired and set up. In fact, in most instances, there is still a lot of hard work ahead. Implementation managers can reduce the time they spend with postinstallation user involvement, depending upon the degree to which clients are consulted at various earlier stages in the adoption process. However, it is important to emphasize that an accurate determination of the ultimate success or failure of an IS largely rests with factors such as system use, user satisfaction, individual impact, and organizational impact. The common denominator underlying each of these factors has to do with the desire to fulfill clients' needs: matching the systems to the clients rather than attempting to alter clients' needs to fit the systems. It behooves installation project managers to spend as much time involved in postintroduction activities as is necessary to better assess the true success or failure of the IS.

Managing a Portfolio of IS Projects—Welcome to the Management-Information-System Zoo

Empirical research shows that IS with higher importance receive more investments, and systems that receive more investments are more successful (Ein-Dor et al. 1984). This was as expected. However, in a sample of ten systems, those with higher importance were actually less successful. This surprising result led to several insights that can guide IS managers in targeting and managing investments in IS systems.

The main insight is that different types of systems exhibit different success dynamics. The three types of IS that explain the negative correlation between importance and success, in decreasing order of perceived success, are easy riders, blockbusters, and Orphan Annies.

EASY RIDERS

Easy riders are systems with moderate levels of importance that achieve high levels of success with low levels of investment. Two of the systems in the sample of ten systems were classified as easy riders because they were the most successful (perceived success of 5.3 on a scale of 1 to 7) in spite of low investment (2.1 on a scale of 1 to 7). These systems were perceived as moderately important (3.2 on a scale of 1 to 7), demonstrating that high levels of success do not require high levels of importance.

These systems are named *easy riders* because they leverage prior investments in IS or in IS infrastructure. For example, executive IS may use existing data collected by transaction-processing systems. Similarly, intranet applications may leverage existing networks and desktop computers to present existing data to employees throughout the organization.

The high success rate of easy riders comes from the fact that they are typically focused on serving very well-defined needs or very few users. The fact that they can be developed quickly and easily contributes to their perceived success as well.

As an IS manager or professional, you should seek and use these types of applications to score early victories and build support for yourself within the organization. There is no shame in seeking big bangs for small bucks.

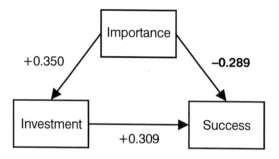

Figure 3.3   Correlations between Importance, Investment, and Success in Information Systems

BLOCKBUSTERS

Blockbusters are systems with high investment, high importance, and medium success. Four of the systems in the sample were classified as blockbusters because they received the highest investment estimates (average of 5.4 on a scale of 1 to 7) and highest importance estimates (average of 5.6 on a scale of 1 to 7). Yet, these systems averaged only a medium level of success (4.2). Here again, the negative correlation between importance and success is evident, since the systems with the highest level of importance are not perceived as the most successful ones.

These systems are called blockbusters because they are large, complex, and very critical. For example, there is a very good chance that the registration system for a university or the MRP system for a manufacturing firm would exhibit these dynamics.

The high importance and investment estimates for these systems are no surprise. The main insight here is that you should expect only a medium level of success from blockbuster systems. On the one hand, the criticality of such systems means that they cannot be complete failures. On the other hand, the complexity of these systems means that they are slow to adapt to changing needs and expectations. Hence, the large user community of blockbuster systems typically generates an ongoing stream of complaints and suggestions for improvements.

As an IS manager or professional, you should come to expect this state of affairs and avoid the temptation to replace blockbuster systems prematurely (see the discussion of SDLC politics in Chapter 6). This does not mean you should turn a deaf ear to complaints and suggestions about blockbuster systems. However, you should realize that while you need to feed and care for your blockbuster systems, this is probably not where you will score major victories in the eyes of the user community. Blockbusters are systems that can cause your early demise, while easy riders are systems that can bring you early glory.

ORPHAN ANNIES

Orphan Annies are systems with low investment, medium to high importance (average of 5.5), and low success (average of 1.6). Two of the systems in the sample were classified as Orphan Annies because they received the lowest investment estimates (average of 1.7) in spite of high importance estimates (average of 5.5). The low investment in these systems explains the name "Orphan Annie" and the very low level of success (average of 1.7 on a scale of 1 to 7). Here, the negative correlation between importance and success is caused by the fact that these systems are important but unsuccessful, due to neglect.

The main insight here is that important systems may not be receiving the attention they deserve. Before drawing your sword and charging to the rescue of these Orphan Annies, you should ask yourself, "Why were these systems neglected so far"? In some cases, neglect was a response to these systems threatening the existing order of things. For example, a system for consolidating detailed financial information across business divisions may threaten the power of divisional managers.

Your assessment of the technical and political readiness surrounding these systems should inform your choice of tactics. If strong political forces oppose the development of the system, you may want to avoid or delay the conflict until you can gather the necessary support of strong organizational champions.

If, on the other hand, the reason for the neglect is more benign, you may want to play a more leading role in pursuing further investments in such systems. For example, some systems may be neglected because so far the technology was not mature enough to handle the challenge in a cost-effective manner.

Recognizing existing and proposed systems as easy riders, blockbusters, or Orphan Annies can allow you to use a better portfolio approach to managing investments in IS projects. At the beginning of your assignment as an IS manager, your portfolio should be biased toward a higher proportion of easy riders in order to score quick and early victories. Later on, you can use the good will and support garnered through these earlier successes in order to address Orphan Annies, and, when appropriate, to replace or overhaul blockbusters. Throughout your tenure, however, you should invest the necessary resources in order to maintain blockbusters in good running condition. A failure of a blockbuster system could be disastrous to the company for which you work and, hence, to your career.

Points to Remember

The discussion in this chapter highlights a number of salient issues that managers need to consider when attempting any sort of system-implementation assessment.

ANY INFORMATION SYSTEM IS ONLY AS GOOD AS IT IS USED

One of the most important points that past research and experience have taught us is that the client is the ultimate determinant of successful system implementation. This lesson, so fundamental to practicing managers, is one that continually escapes the attention of researchers and IS theoreticians and must be continually relearned. We continue to deal with a culture that is fascinated with the latest technological advances. One has only to pick up a newspaper or business magazine to read of the widespread influence of the impending *information superhighway*, despite the fact that the average person may be over a decade away from realizing many of the practical benefits of this family of technologies. In our drive to innovate, there is a very real danger that we will begin to pursue technology for technology's sake, rather than working to create systems that have practical and useful features. The oft-repeated statement—"Of course it will be used; it's state of the art!"—reveals a high level of naiveté about how innovations are received and perceived by the average person. Project managers need to devote as much time to networking with potential clients as they do with ensuring that all the technical features of a new IS are performing well.

SUCCESSFUL IMPLEMENTATION MAY REQUIRE SYSTEM AND CLIENT MODIFICATION

A fundamental finding of Schultz and Slevin's earlier work referred to the concept of organizational validity (1979). What is important about this concept is the implication that any new IS must be *right* for the organization toward which it is targeted. Further, the right system refers to the importance of matching the needs and attitudes of the client organization to the new technology. Many firms acquire IS that are underutilized because they are inappropriate for the target organization. However, it is important that the reader understand that an inappropriate system is often not the direct result of technical difficulties or performance-characteristic flaws. Many times, an IS will be perceived as inappropriate because it does not conform to the attitudes and value systems of the majority of organizational members. In other words, the cultural ambiance of a firm must be taken into consideration when determining its technological needs.

The process of developing greater organizational validity for an IS innovation involves a process of mutual adaptation between the system and the client organization. Significant preplanning is required from the project manager and team members, as they scan the client and objectively assess attitudes and needs regarding an IS. If the team determines that it is not feasible to implement an IS within the current organizational context, it needs to begin formulating plans for how to create a more supportive environment. That process may require either modifying the IS to suit the technological needs of the company, engaging in large-scale training programs within the company to create an atmosphere of acceptance, or both. Unless project managers and their teams work to address potential problems of organizational validity, their highly developed and technically sophisticated systems are likely to fail without having been given a sufficient chance to succeed.

WHEN ASSESSING SUCCESS, GIVE THE SYSTEM TIME TO BE INCORPORATED INTO THE CLIENT'S OPERATIONS

A common feature of determining project success is to evaluate the process from a primarily internal perspective. We typically assess how successful our projects are by using the triple constraint as the metric: adherence to budget and schedule and conformance to specifications. In assessing the performance of an IS implementation, however, project managers are faced with a significantly more complex task. Because so much depends upon the acceptance and use of the system and its resultant impact on the client organization's operations, it is foolish to continue to rely on internal measures of project success. Rather, we need to broaden our definition to include elements of systems' impact, for it is by this measure that project managers can gain a true sense of the efficacy of the implementation effort.

The obvious difficulty with making any sort of post hoc impact assessment is that of determining when best to make such an analysis. In other words, how long should a system be in place before it is analyzed for its utility to firm operations? Any new system will require a shakedown period, while clients learn how to use it and adapt it to their activities. At the same time, they are also likely to be learning the various strong and weak points of the IS, and, hence, are usually unable to formulate an accurate assessment of the system for some time. On the other hand, the longer they take to assess implementation and performance success, the greater the likelihood that other intervening variables will interfere with their abilities to give honest appraisals of the IS. For example, as new technological breakthroughs occur, any current IS will begin to look old and increasingly cumbersome to its users, particularly when compared to the capabilities that new systems offer. Further, just as it is wrong to link a project manager's performance assessment or bonuses to internal measures of success, it is equally unfair to reschedule the review for some nebulous time in the future when success can be more accurately measured.

Clearly, a tradeoff must be made between assessing implementation success too quickly and waiting too long. Whatever decision rule is adopted by the project manager's superiors, they need to make it with due regard for the various tradeoffs that exist, and the decision criteria must be applied consistently across all projects of a similar nature.

Conclusions

Much has been written and continues to be produced in efforts to develop a better and simpler model of IS success. Any efforts toward establishing a unifying model must question certain aspects of the system itself. Does it work? Is it technically valid and usable? Further, unless the IS is used in organizational activities and becomes an integral part of the organization's operations, its impact is bound to be lessened. Finally, the bottom line of any newly installed system lies in its impact on individual and organizational operations, in spite of the difficulties involved in attempting to develop an accurate and generalizable metric of IS impact.

This chapter offers a framework around which the various ideas of IS success could be analyzed. It is necessary to note that managers and readers who are currently content with their systems, regardless of their inability to measure up to several of the success determinants noted here, need to regularly conduct a reevaluation of their IS and assess their true centrality to their departments' missions and operations. Unless due care is taken to ensure that an IS can be positively evaluated according to the criteria established here, it is unlikely that it is living up to its full potential and, for that matter, neither is the using department reaching its full potential.

4

Critical Success Factors in Information System Projects

> But Lord, to see what success do, whether with or without reason,
> [in] making a man seem wise.
>
> *Samuel Pepys*

Managers charged with successful implementation of new information systems (IS) face a number of challenges today in their management tasks. The environment of organizations is becoming more dynamic with increasing uncertainties in technology, budgets, and development processes. Highly trained and well-educated experts must be coordinated, so that their technical inputs and expertise integrate well into the human system in which they are operating. Thus, the manager charged with successful implementation of an IS must be increasingly aware of any early warning signs of problems, either technical or organizational in nature. Project managers should also be aware of some of the wide range of issues, termed critical success factors (CSFs), that play a significant role in determining the likelihood of implementation success or failure. Numerous computer-software management aids have been developed (and will later be discussed) to help manage the technical aspects of projects (interdependencies, budgets, schedules, and so forth). However, CSF offer IS managers an important tool in assessing the behavioral and organizational aspects of implementation—aspects of at least equal importance to implementation success, as are the more technically based factors.

Currently, most managers of implementation efforts attend to these CSF in an intuitive and ad hoc fashion, as they attempt to manage and allocate their time and resources across a number of conflicting demands. A more refined and specific model of these CSF and their interrelationships would help achieve success. Research in recent years has provided an approach to the measurement of these factors to assist IS managers in allocating resources and detecting problem areas early enough to respond in an effective manner. This chapter describes a framework of CSF for the implementation of IS technology.

The Research

CSF are those factors that, if adequately tended, will significantly improve the chances for successful new system implementation. Several authors, writing on the implementation process, especially in the area of IS project implementation, have developed sets of CSF. This chapter will focus on three of the better-known streams of CSF research and their implications for IS implementation. The first study, using a sample of British firms, looks at major drivers and inhibitors of project success (Morris 1983). The other two studies, by Baker et al. (1988) and J. K. Pinto and Slevin (1988a), examine the CSF for implementation success using samples of projects from United States companies.

Although all of these research studies focus on project implementation in general (including examples of IS projects but not limited to them exclusively), commonalties between the projects studied and the characteristics of IS implementation make the findings highly relevant to our discussion. After all, more than anything else, IS implementation is a project. While examining these findings, note the high level of agreement that exists among the findings in these studies, regardless of the different implementation efforts being studied and the potential cultural differences that exist.

THE MORRIS STUDY

The first study was based on a large sample of British firms and their efforts at implementing new technologies (Morris 1983). The key concept derived from this study was the breakdown of the implementation process into a life cycle comprising four stages: 1) team formation, 2) build-up, 3) main phase, and, 4) closeout. Among the behavioral factors examined by the study were personal motivation, top management support, team motivation, clear objectives, client support, technical issues, and financial concerns. The results of the study, as shown in Table 4.1, demonstrate three important points. First, the relative importance of the various CSF changes as the implementation effort proceeds through its life cycle. For example, at stage one, team formation, the most important factors are personal motivation and top management support. However, by the time the implementation process is in its closeout stage, personal and team motivation have become the most important factors affecting the success of the project.

The second point is that behavioral and organizational factors far outweigh technical (or process) issues in terms of their importance for implementation success. Rather than focusing undue concern on process issues (adequate budgets, financial support, scheduling, and so forth), this study argues that it is far more important to pay attention to the human side of the implementation process. It also stresses that management does not simply imply oversight but also attendance to the needs and concerns of members of the implementation team, as well as the clients.

The final point, closely related to the other two issues, is to note that these human and organizational issues, which are the primary drivers of implementation success, can also have significant impact on system failure if not addressed. Table 4.2 demonstrates that the inhibitors of successful implementation, once again, are clearly shown to be primarily behavioral and organizational in nature, rather than technical.

THE BAKER, MURPHY, AND FISHER STUDY

The Morris study sparked interest in the analysis of CSF within the project implementation context partially because it pointed clearly to the critical role that behavioral and organizational factors can play in the successful implementation of innovations. A separate study by Baker, Murphy, and Fisher addressed a comprehensive list of those factors that were thought to contribute to perceived project-implementation success (1983). Their list also included a number of behavioral dimensions (project team spirit, project team and leader goal commitment, project manager's human skills, job security of implementation team, and so forth). It also included organizational issues (parent organization enthusiasm, satisfaction with project team structure, adequacy of change procedures, and so forth) and technical factors (development of a realistic budget and schedule to completion, technical details of the system to be implemented, and so forth). They examined over 650 projects across a wide range of project types, durations, budgeted costs, and goals.

As Table 4.3 shows, the similarity of their findings to the earlier British study are striking. The column labeled Standardized Regression Coefficient refers to the beta coefficient, measuring strength of linear relationship between each of the variables and project success. Cumulative R-square measures the predictive power of each of the variables in determining the likelihood of project success. Again, the behavioral and organizational

Principal Success Drivers	
Stage	**Critical Success Factors (in order of importance)**
Formation	Personal Ambition
	Top Management Support
	Team Motivation
	Clear Objectives
	Technological Advantage
Build-up	Team Motivation
	Personal Motivation
	Top Management Support
	Technical Expertise
Main Phase	Team Motivation
	Personal Motivation
	Client Support
	Top Management Support
Close-out	Personal Motivation
	Team Motivation
	Top Management Support
	Financial Support

From Morris (1983)

Table 4.1   Findings from the British Study on Critical Success Factors, Part I

factors are clearly most important. In particular, the single factor of Coordination and Team-Client Relations—encompassing a variety of items, such as capability of the project team, sense of mission, team spirit, goal commitment, and supportive informal relations of team members—accounted by itself for 77 percent of the contributors of implementation success.

These two studies illustrate that any discussion of the factors critical for system-implementation success must look beyond the basic technical

Principal Inhibitors to Success	
Stage	**Problems with Critical Success Factors (in order of importance)**
Formation	Unmotivated Team
	Poor Leadership
	Technical Limitations
	Money
Build-up	Unmotivated Team
	Conflict in Objectives
	Leadership Problems
	Poor Top Management Support
	Technical Problems
Main Phase	Unmotivated Team
	Poor Top Management Support
	Deficient Procedures
Close-out	Poor Control
	Poor Financial Support
	Objectives
	Leadership

From Morris (1983)

Table 4.2   Findings from the British Study on Critical Success Factors, Part II

merits of the system. Too often, particularly among technical personnel, there is a tendency to see problems and possibilities from a narrowly focused perspective. In implementing an IS, managers placed in charge of that process must acknowledge that mastery of the technical aspects of the system provides, in itself, no guarantee of adoption success. In fact, such mastery may actually hurt the prospects for successful introduction if it influences the manager to overemphasize technical issues over the human side of the project management process.

Standardized Regression			
Determining Factors	Coefficient	Significance	Cumulative R-Square
Coordination and Team-Client Relations	+.35	p < .001	.773
Adequacy of Team Structure and Control	+.19	p < .001	.830
System Uniqueness, Importance, and Public Exposure	+.15	p < .001	.887
Success Criteria Salience and Consensus	+.25	p < .001	.886
Competitive and Budgetary Pressure	−.15	p < .001	.897
Initial Over-Optimism, Conceptual Difficulty	−.22	p < .001	.905
Internal Capabilities Build-up	+.08	p < .001	.911

From Baker, Murphy, and Fisher (1988)

Table 4.3   Factors Contributing to Perceived Implementation Success

THE PINTO AND SLEVIN STUDY

These two authors conducted a more recent study of CSF in the project-implementation process, examining over four hundred projects varying greatly in terms of basic characteristics (1988a). A wide range of representative samples of project types included R&D, construction, information system, and so forth. This study validated a ten-factor model of CSF for project implementation, as illustrated in Table 4.4. Further, J. K. Pinto and Slevin also confirmed the importance of managerial, behavioral, and organizational issues in successful system implementation. In fact, this research determined that, to a large degree, these CSF remained within the control of the project manager responsible for implementing the IS. Therefore, by attending to these CSF rather than being held captive by a chain of events beyond their control, project managers have a strong capacity to influence and improve their teams' chances of implementation success. Following a more detailed discussion of Pinto and Slevin's list of CSF, a synopsis of their research findings as they pertain to system implementation will be discussed.

Critical Success Factors—A Ten-Factor Model

As the previous section demonstrates, there is a growing body of project management literature that focuses on implementation CSF. However, in many cases, project management prescriptions and process frameworks are theoretically based rather than empirically proven. That is, the evidence supporting these sets of factors often comprises anecdotal, single-case studies, or they are theory derived rather than empirical. While sometimes there exists strong intuitive evidence supporting the conceptual frameworks of the project management process, there is relatively little empirical basis for the resulting models and theories of project management and implementation. From Pinto and Slevin's research and development of a ten-factor model (1987), however, we can begin to explore how these factors offer new insights into the *managerial* nature of project CSF.

FACTOR DEFINITIONS

Project mission relates to the underlying purpose for the implementation. Several authors have discussed the importance of clearly defining objectives, as well as ultimate benefits to be derived from the project. For example, Morris classified the initial stage of project management as consisting of a feasibility decision (1983). Are the objectives clear, and can they succeed? For these authors and the purposes of our study, Project Mission refers to a condition where the objectives of the project are clear and understood, not only by the project team involved, but also by the other departments in the organization. Sample issues for project managers to consider under this factor include: "The basic objectives of the project are clear to me and the project team," and, "The objectives of the project are in line with the general objectives of the organization." The project manager must be concerned with clarification of objectives, as well as achieving broad belief in the congruence of the objectives with overall organizational objectives.

Top management support, the second factor, has long been considered of great importance in distinguishing between project success or failure. Beck sees project management as not only dependent upon top management

1. Project Mission

Initial clearly defined goals and general directions.

2. Top Management Support

Willingness of top management to provide the necessary resources and authority/power for implementation success.

3. Schedule/Plans

Detailed specification of the individual action steps for system implementation.

4. Client Consultation

Communication, consultation, and active listening to all parties impacted by the proposed information system.

5. Personnel

Recruitment, selection, and training of the necessary personnel for the implementation project team.

6. Technical Tasks

Availability of the required technology and expertise to accomplish the specific technical action steps to bring the information system online.

7. Client Acceptance

Act of *selling* the final product to its ultimate intended users.

8. Monitoring and Feedback

Timely provision of comprehensive control information at each stage in the implementation process.

9. Communication

Provision of an appropriate network and necessary data to all key actors in the information system implementation process.

10. Troubleshooting

Ability to handle unexpected crises and deviations from plan.

Table 4.4   Factor Definitions

for authority, direction, and support but also as the conduit for implementing top management's plans or goals for the organization (1983). Further, the degree of management support for a project will lead to significant variations in the degree of acceptance or resistance to that project or product. Top management's support of the project may involve aspects such as allocation of sufficient resources (including financial, manpower, time, and so on), as well as project management's confidence in top management's support in the event of crisis. Sample statements to consider when addressing this factor include, "I agree with upper management on the extent of my authority and degree of responsibility for the project," and, "I have the confidence of upper management."

Project plans and schedules refers to the importance of developing a detailed plan of the required stages of the implementation process. It is important, however, to bear in mind that the actual activities associated with planning and project scheduling are distinct from each other. Planning is comprised of scope definition, creation of a work breakdown structure, and resource and activity assignments. It is the first and more general step in developing the project-implementation strategy. Scheduling is the setting of the time frames and milestones for each important element in the overall project.

Project plans and schedules also refers to the degree to which time schedules, milestones, labor, and equipment requirements are specified. There must be a satisfactory measurement system to judge actual performance against budget allowances and time schedules. A sample of the type of statements considered in this factor include, "I have identified the important labor skills required for successful project completion," and, "I have contingency plans in case the project gets off schedule."

Client consultation was determined to be the fourth factor. The *client* is anyone who will ultimately be making use of the product of the project, as either a customer outside the company or a department within the organization. The need for client consultation has been found to be increasingly important in attempting a successful system implementation. Indeed, Manley found that the degree to which clients are personally involved in the implementation process correlates directly with the variation in their support for that project (1975). It is important to identify the clients for the project and accurately determine if their needs are being met. Some examples of statements contained in the Client Consultation factor include, "I have solicited input from all potential clients of the IS," and "I understand the needs of those who will use the system."

The fifth factor, *personnel*, includes recruitment, selection, and training. An important but often overlooked aspect of the implementation process concerns the nature of the personnel involved. In many situations, personnel for the project team are chosen with less than full regard for the skills necessary to actively contribute to implementation success. Some current writers on implementation are including the personnel variable in their equations for project team success. For example, one researcher has developed a contingency model of the implementation process, which includes "people" as a situational variable whose knowledge, skills, goals, and personalities must be considered in assessing the environment of the organization (Hammond III 1979). For our framework, Personnel, as a factor, is concerned with developing an implementation team with the ability and commitment to perform its function. Examples of statements for the Personnel factor include, "The personnel of my project team are committed to the system's success," and, "The lines of authority are well defined on my project team."

Technical tasks refers to the necessity of having not only the required numbers of personnel for the implementation team, but also ensuring that they possess technical skills and have the necessary technology and technical support to perform their tasks. It is important that the implementation be managed by people who understand the technology involved. In addition, there must exist adequate technology to support the system. Examples of technical task statements include, "The technology that is being implemented works well," and, "Experts, consultants, or other experienced managers outside the project team have reviewed and criticized my basic plans and approach."

Client acceptance refers to the final stage in the implementation process, at which time the overall efficacy of the project is to be determined. In addition to client consultation at an earlier stage in the system-implementation process, it remains of ultimate importance to determine whether the clients for whom the project has been initiated will accept it. Too often, project managers make the mistake of believing that if they handle the other stages of the implementation process well, the client (either internal or external to the organization) will accept the resulting system. In fact, several writers have shown that client acceptance is a stage in project implementation that must be managed like any other. Some researchers have even proposed the use of "intermediaries" to act as a liaison between the designer, or implementation team, and the project's potential users to aid in client acceptance (Bean and Radnor 1979). Examples of statements referring to Client Acceptance include: "Potential clients have been contacted about the usefulness of the IS," and, "Adequate advanced preparation has been done to determine how best to 'sell' the project to clients."

The eighth factor to be considered is that of *monitoring and feedback*, which refers to the project control process by which, at each stage of the project implementation, key personnel receive feedback on how the project is progressing, compared to initial projections. Making allowances for adequate monitoring and feedback mechanisms gives the project manager the ability to anticipate problems, oversee corrective measures, and ensure that no deficiencies are overlooked. Project managers need to emphasize the importance of constant monitoring and fine-tuning the process of implementation. For our model, Monitoring and Feedback refers not only to project schedule and budget, but also to monitoring performance of members of the project team. Sample statements for the Monitoring and Feedback factor include, "When the budget or schedule requires revision, I solicit input from the project team," and, "All members of the project team know if I am satisfied or dissatisfied with their work."

Communication channels are extremely important in creating an atmosphere for successful system implementation. Communication is not only essential within the project team itself but also between the team and the rest of the organization, as well as with the clients. Figure 4.1 demonstrates the tripartite nature of communication and the necessity of keeping open channels among all active stakeholders in the IS' development. The communication factor refers not only to feedback mechanisms, but also to the necessity of exchanging information with both clients and the rest of the organization concerning the IS' capabilities, goals of the implementation process, changes in policies and procedures, status reports, and so forth. Some examples of the type of issues that are of concern for Communication include, "Input concerning the implementation effort's goals and strategy have been sought from members of the project team, other groups affected by the IS, and upper management," and, "All groups affected by the system know how to make problems known to those who can deal with them."

Troubleshooting is the tenth and final factor of the model. Problem areas exist in almost every implementation. The measure of a successful implementation effort is not the avoidance of problems, but knowing the correct steps to take once problems develop. Regardless of how carefully the implementation effort was initially planned, it is impossible to foresee every trouble area or problem that could possibly arise. As a result, it is important for the project manager to make adequate arrangements to recognize problems and for troubleshooting mechanisms to be included in the implementation plan. Such mechanisms would make it easier to not only react to problems as they arise, but also to foresee and possibly forestall potential problem areas in the implementation process. One of the best and most pragmatic mechanisms is to follow the dictum of *management by walking around*. It is only through direct and frequent interaction with all project stakeholders—including the team, top management, and the clients—that project managers develop the day-to-day *flavor* of the project, including a sense of where potential problems are likely to arise. Some examples of issues to be considered under the

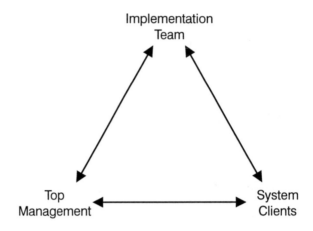

Figure 4.1   The Three-Way Path of Communication

Troubleshooting factor include, "I spend a part of each day looking for problems that have just begun or have the potential to begin," and, "Implementation team members are encouraged to take quick, personal action on problems on their own initiative."

What Should Information System Professionals Do?

Three research efforts on the ten-factor model are described briefly at the end of this chapter, and the results of this research are summarized in the following conclusions.

KEEP THE MISSION IN THE FOREFRONT

On the surface, it seems obvious to state that it is important to keep the mission in mind when implementing an IS. However, the point bears repeating and underlining. Research on the ten-factor model demonstrates clearly that adherence to the mission was the number-one cause of implementation success. Remember that *mission* refers to not simply having a mission to implement the IS, but also conveying exactly what the objectives of the implementation effort are to all concerned parties, particularly the other project team members and prospective users of the system.

- What will the IS do for us?
- How long do we expect it to take to install and bring it online?
- Does every member of the project team understand and buy into these objectives?

These are just some of the important questions that need to be asked about the mission of the IS implementation. Nothing will derail a new system implementation faster than not having clearly communicated the objectives of the project to all groups impacted by the IS. When objectives change or need updating, that information also needs to be made public.

One well-known problem with bringing new systems online is the potential for *mission creep*—that is, the project's goals begin to change as the project progresses. There are many examples of IS that for whatever reason underwent major specification, technological or user changes, or got off on such tangents that the originally agreed-upon system objectives became meaningless. Obviously, some modifications are bound to occur as a system is customized for a particular organization's uses. However, the underlying purpose of the IS must remain clear and important for all members of the implementation project team and the clients.

CONSULT WITH YOUR CLIENTS EARLY

Remember that *clients* refers to any planned or potential user of the system. Regardless of who the client is for a particular project, it should be apparent that consultation and communication with clients throughout the acquisition and installation of the IS are very important for its successful implementation. Put another way, one of the worst things that an IS manager can do is acquire and install a system without engaging in any meaningful dialogue with the departments that could potentially make use of the technology. There is an old saying that "people don't mind 'change,' they just don't like being changed." We tend to be leery of anything that can cause disruption in our thought patterns, approaches to decision-making, or work habits. An IS is bound to cause disruptions in all three of these areas. Therefore, knowing in advance that this new technology is destined to change departmental operations forever (in a positive manner, it is hoped), it makes excellent sense to spend a considerable amount of time up-front laying the groundwork for successful introduction of the IS.

STAY WELL CONNECTED TO CLIENTS

Client acceptance, a selling activity, is necessary during the initial planning processes, as well as during the termination phase of the implementation. Often, the sequence of operations concerned with the client follows the pattern of: 1) consult to determine specific needs, 2) sell ideas (including the benefits of IS technology), budgets, and time frame to completion, and, 3) perform a final verification of client acceptance once the project

Factor	Beta	t-Value	Sig. t
Mission	.72	19.99	$p < .001$
Top Management Support	.32	10.60	$p < .001$
Schedule	.32	10.92	$p < .001$
Client Consultation	.39	11.86	$p < .001$
Personnel	.31	10.54	$p < .001$
Technical Tasks	.43	11.25	$p < .001$
Client Acceptance	.39	11.46	$p < .001$
Monitoring and Feedback	.29	10.89	$p < .001$
Communication	.32	10.38	$p < .001$
Troubleshooting	.35	11.15	$p < .001$

Cumulative $R2 = .615**$

* Beta refers to the strength of the relationship between the predictor variable and project success. As the model demonstrates, while all the variables are strongly related to project success, Mission has the highest impact, based on its beta value of .72.

** Refers to the predictive power of the model. An r-square value of 1.0 would be perfectly predictive.

From J. K. Pinto and Slevin (1988a)

Table 4.5   Critical Success Factors and Their Importance for System Implementation

has been completed. This verification may be in the form of a series of formal demonstrations of the IS for departments intended to use it.

In developing and implementing an IS technology, do not underestimate the importance of selling the technology to the clients, even after having initially consulted with them about the system. An important truth concerning the implementation of IS suggests that one can never talk to the clients enough. A corollary to that rule argues that just because the IS manager and implementation team members have once spent time consulting with clients about the system, it is absolutely incorrect to now assume that clients will embrace the finished product with open arms. In the time between initial consultation and installation, too much can change that will alter their perceptions of the system. The technology may be altered significantly. A great deal of time may have elapsed, changing the basic reasons for even needing the system. One of the department's chief proponents of IS may have since left to take another job. The common denominator of all these issues is that time does not stand still between initial client consultation and final IS installation. Do not automatically assume that you fully understand the client's concerns or, that having installed the system, it will now be used.

Increasingly, organizations are developing methods aimed at improving links to clients. The process, referred to sometimes as *external integration*, makes use of a number of alternative methods, including creating mixed developer and client teams, prototyping, and creating quality circles, all with the intent of improving the lines of communication between builders and customers. Once these integrated teams are developed, they play a key role in the subsequent *selling* of the IS project to its intended user base.

Make Sure You Have Adequate Technology to Succeed

The successful installation and adoption of an IS assumes that the organization has the technology or the technically capable people to support the system and ensure that it succeeds. Many small children suffer from the "eyes-bigger-than-the stomach" syndrome. This malady manifests itself most often at mealtimes, particularly during dessert. No matter how much the child may have eaten to that point, once dessert is offered, it is almost always accepted. Of course, there is no guarantee that it will be eaten; in fact, it is rarely completely finished. The children are simply manifesting the eyes-bigger-than-the-stomach behavior.

This point illustrates a similar characteristic with many organizations; they too suffer from eyes bigger than the stomach. A new technology is introduced nationally, and someone within the organization develops great enthusiasm for the technology. The question that needs to be asked at this point is whether or not the organization can support the successful introduction of this new technology with the personnel and facilities it currently possesses. If the answer is no, the organization needs to take immediate remedial steps—either hiring additional support personnel with the necessary technical backgrounds, instituting a departmentwide training program to bring potential users up to technical standards, or, if necessary, put the brakes on the system's introduction until another time when it can be more fully supported.

It is just as important that the project team not become obsessed with state-of-the-art technology. It is better to have a solid, working solution than to have all the latest technology in a nonworking, nonused system or to have interminable delays in getting the system operational.

SET UP AND MAINTAIN A SCHEDULING AND CONTROL SYSTEM

Implementation planning is an activity that many IS managers would rather avoid. The process can sometimes be rather tedious and often does not yield any immediate, visible results. Nevertheless, it is impossible to underestimate the importance of comprehensive and detailed planning for successful IS implementation. There is great validity to the old saying, "Those who fail to plan are planning to fail."

When can planning be most effective? Obviously, during the early start-up of the implementation effort, planning is paramount. This type of planning involves breaking down the specific work activities into meaningful bits (using a work breakdown structure), setting milestones, and assigning the necessary personnel to tackle each of these duties. However, planning is also very useful during the termination phase of the IS introduction. First, schedules provide feedback on how well the project team accomplished its goals while also providing a learning device through comparing projected schedules with actual results. Second, schedules are needed for the transfer of the system to its intended users. Transferring the project, establishing training sessions and maintenance cycles, and getting it online usually require an additional series of target dates and schedules.

PUT THE RIGHT PEOPLE ON THE PROJECT TEAM

The results of the research demonstrate the importance of recruiting, selecting, and training people who possess the necessary technical and administrative skills to positively influence the ultimate success of the IS installation. Does the organization currently possess the people capable of understanding the technology and dealing with the headaches, deadlines, and conflict that an implementation project can bring? Of equal importance is the question, "How are project team members assigned to the group?" In many organizations, members are assigned to project teams purely on an availability basis. If managers have subordinates who are currently free, these people are put on the team, regardless of whether or not they possess the technical qualifications, people skills, or administrative abilities to perform effectively. In some organizations, the picture is even worse. Oftentimes, individuals are assigned to projects not based on their positive capabilities, but as transfers to move them out of their departments and make them someone else's problem. In these cases, managers, dealing with problem subordinates, simply use the project as an excuse to ship their troublemakers to other assignments. It is easy to imagine the prospects for projects that are continually staffed with castoffs and incompetents. Personnel, as a CSF, implies having and assigning the most qualified individuals to the implementation team, not the most available. We owe IS technology more than to simply make an implementation team the dumping ground for malcontents.

MAKE SURE TOP MANAGEMENT GETS BEHIND THE SYSTEM

It is well accepted that top management can either help or hinder a project such as a new system introduction. Top management grants the necessary authority to the IS manager, controls needed resources, arbitrates cross-departmental disputes, and rewards the final results. Its role in the successful implementation of a new system should not be overlooked. However, top-management support must go further than simply approving the new system. Statements of support have to be backed by concrete actions and demonstrations of loyalty. Actions speak far louder than words and have a way of truly demonstrating how top management feels about the system. Are members of top management putting their money where their mouths are, or is their support simply pro forma? This is an important question that needs to be resolved early in the implementation process, before significant time and resources have been spent.

Further, top management's support can be most critical when the actual work of the implementation is being done rather than early on, or after the system is online. Top management is most able at this point to make its presence felt through providing the necessary money, personnel, and support for the system, as they are needed. Finally, both IS managers and their teams need to know that top management will support them in the event of unforeseen difficulties or crises. All implementation efforts encounter difficulties but *fair-weather* supporters at the top can be terribly demoralizing.

CONTINUALLY ASK THE "WHAT IF?" QUESTIONS

It is axiomatic that problems will occur with the implementation effort. All projects run into trouble, and the mark of a successful project manager is not one who can foresee and forestall problems; rather, the successful project manager is the individual who has taken the time to puzzle out appropriate responses to likely trouble spots. Troubleshooting is particularly appropriate in the implementation of an IS because there are so many human and technical variables that can go wrong. The project manager has to be cognizant of technical issues and difficulties that can arise, but it is usually the behavioral and organizational issues that are more common, pressing, and potentially damaging to implementation success. Therefore, the act of simply troubleshooting the technical features of the IS will be of only limited usefulness.

One final point about troubleshooting needs to be mentioned. We have already discussed the importance of a clear project mission for successful implementation. In fact, it was noted as the number-one contributor to project success. A follow-up study was conducted by J. K. Pinto and Mantel to investigate—again using the-ten factor model—the principal contributors to implementation failure (1990). In that study, the number-one cause of failure in project implementation was a lack of adequate troubleshooting mechanisms. Follow-up interviews supported their findings: Managers who had spent extra time early in the project establishing contingency plans were less often caught by surprise, spent less time puzzling their responses, and got their projects back on track faster than those who ignored troubleshooting and did not ask the "What if?" questions. The projects that were viewed as unsuccessful due to poor adherence to schedule, budget, performance specifications, and user acceptance were almost always associated with an inadequate or nonexistent attempt by the project team at troubleshooting.

One example of a company promoting this what-if thinking is a large Midwestern telecommunications firm that routinely involves top management in project-planning sessions. Members of top management act as devil's advocates in project meetings by challenging the assumptions that underlie all planning and operational decisions. The process has evolved to the point when members of project teams have now been unofficially designated to play this role with other team members, so that all operational decisions must first pass through several levels of constructive criticism prior to initiation.

Improving the Quality of the Analysis Phase— Three Silver Bullets

It is well accepted that poor analysis is responsible for many IS project fiascoes. The common failure to identify the system requirements correctly and completely is an expensive and often fatal mistake.

A variety of methodologies and software tools—such as structured systems analysis, joint application design, prototyping, computer-aided software engineering, and object-oriented analysis—aim at improving the quality of the requirements' specifications. Rather than reviewing these comprehensive approaches, we would like to focus attention on three low-cost techniques that can lead to higher-quality analysis.

DEVIL'S ADVOCATE

Research indicates that conflict-based techniques such as devil's advocacy and dialectical inquiry are effective in improving the quality of decisions and problem solving (Schweiger et al. 1989; Schwenk 1990a, 1990b; Valacich and Schwenk 1995). Our own experience shows that subjecting requirements-specification documents to a review by an independent devil's advocate is an extremely effective method for detecting problems and improving the quality of the analysis phase.

Although devil's advocacy is a well-known technique, many IS project managers fail to use it early enough in the project life cycle. The products of the detailed design phase may undergo a "Critical Design Review," and the actual programming code may be subjected to "Inspections" and "Structured Walkthrough" (Freedman and Weinberg 1990). However, the earlier feasibility and analysis phases typically lack similar rigorous reviews.

The feasibility study and the requirements specifications are typically reviewed by steering committees and user departments, and such reviews are indeed essential. However, these reviews lack two key aspects of a devil's advocate review: 1) the explicit focus on uncovering flaws, and, 2) the involvement of an external reviewer who sees the analysis from a fresh perspective, and who is not invested in the process so far. An external IS professional who is invited to act as a devil's advocate can save the project team from embarrassing mistakes found during the internal reviews, or even more costly mistakes that go undetected until well into the implementation and deployment phases.

Since the documents produced during the earlier phases of the project are relatively short, the devil's advocate's review requires only a brief time commitment. This means that you can afford requesting this service from consultants or from other experienced IS professionals within your organization. This type of short engagement may also fit the schedule constraints of IS faculty members at local universities. You may even strike a devil's-advocate reciprocity deal with the IS department of another local organization.

This brings us to one more source for improving the quality of the analysis phase.

OTHER ORGANIZATIONS

There is a very good chance that your project shares some similarities with other projects that were already tackled by other organizations. It might require the introduction of the same technology, the use of the same software package, the development of similar functionality, or the transition to similar new work processes. You can learn a lot from the experience of those other organizations.

Yet, this source of excellent information is frequently ignored by IS professionals. Our experience indicates that most IS professionals think that requesting this type of information is more difficult than it really is. What these IS professionals fail to realize is that the IS professional on the other end of the phone line has a variety of reasons for cooperating with a request for such information. Besides being able to brag and talk about their wonderful systems, IS professionals may respond positively to such requests because they recognize them as opportunities for networking, information sharing, consulting, and even new jobs.

In short, calling other organizations for useful information is typically easier than you might think. You have very little to lose and much to gain if you can overcome the fear of rejection and the *not-invented-here* syndrome. Besides getting useful information that can save you much time, cost, and embarrassment, these information-exchange processes offer you networking opportunities as well.

Information exchange with other organizations becomes a particularly obvious technique when your project involves the selection of a software package. The vendor of the software package should be willing to provide you with a list of contacts in other organizations, who are already using the package. In such package-oriented projects, the following technique can provide additional help in improving the quality and reducing the cost of the analysis phase.

Feature mapping. Textbooks and seminars on how requirements analysis should be conducted typically emphasize the identification of requirements via techniques such as user interviews and joint-application-design meetings. The role of the analyst in such interviews and meetings is to identify, organize, and prioritize user needs. It sounds easy enough, but in reality this process can be difficult.

The problem is that this process requires a high level of conceptualization and cooperation from both analysts and users. Imagine you are an analyst who is approaching an office manager of an insurance agency with the question, "What do you need from an insurance-agency management software?" It is cognitively difficult to respond to such a question. It forces the user to imagine or recall various scenarios and formulate system requirements around these scenarios. Although some scenarios or needs can be quite obvious, others may be left undetected with this type of unaided recall process.

From the point of view of the office manager, the analyst has just dumped a very challenging question on the table without showing any domain knowledge. The internal dialogue could be something like the following:

> This kid who's making three times my salary and knows absolutely nothing about insurance is asking me to do his work for him. I'm not going to put an ounce of extra effort into this beyond the absolute minimum of looking like I'm cooperating.

You may attempt to use a variety of techniques such as diagrams and event-focused interviewing in order to break down the cognitive challenge into manageable pieces. However, the underlying process still requires some level of unaided recall from the user, who may be less than delighted to interact with an analyst who comes across as ignorant about the domain.

Feature mapping is a technique that can frequently address this problem, leading to better definition of system requirements in less time and with a more positive interaction between the systems analyst and the user.

Textbook approaches to requirements specification would lead you to believe that even when you aim to select a software package as a solution, you should go through the process of analyzing the system requirements before embarking on the process of identifying and evaluating the candidate packages. The logic behind this suggestion is: You should know what you need before you go buying it. It sounds reasonable, but in our opinion it is a naive, wasteful, and even dangerous prescription.

According to the feature-mapping approach, before you identify the system requirements, you should identify several software packages that address the application domain you are investigating. You then combine the various services and features offered by these packages into a list of potential requirements. The longer the list, the more structure you need to impose on it in order to keep it coherent. For example, you may want to break it into sections and subsections, according to the way these features map to organizational users, organizational levels, functional areas, or business processes.

Each service or feature on this list is a potential requirement that the users may need from the system. As Table 4.6 shows, you should maintain information about which of the packages offers each of the services.

As shown in the last two columns of Table 4.6, you should use this list to ask the users how much they need each of the features. In this example, a 5 denotes absolute *must have*, and a 0 indicates *not needed*. For the users, this is a much easier question to answer, and the analyst comes across as knowledgeable about the domain. Obviously, before this interviewing process, the analyst should investigate the meaning of any features that seem obscure.

During the interview process, the discussion of features on the list may trigger in the mind of the user additional needs. Such new requirements should be added to the list, and subsequent discussions with the software vendors should assess if these services are included in the package or can be easily added.

This simple process can make the analysis phase before selecting a software package faster, more complete, and more enjoyable. Furthermore, the results of this process are already in a format that supports the selection of the top package and the communication of the rationale for that choice.

In complex situations, you can assign importance levels to each feature in the list and assess how well each package addresses that requirement. These estimates can be used in a scoring table, or an analytic-hierarchy-process model, to support a more sophisticated ranking of candidate packages. We provide a detailed discussion of these techniques in the context of prioritizing IS projects in Chapter 5.

Finally, it should be noted that feature mapping can be used to facilitate and improve the process of requirements specification, even in situations when you believe that existing software packages do not offer a viable solution.

Conclusions

This chapter focuses on the results of recent research and its implications for successful IS implementation using CSF. The interest in CSF as a methodology for gaining better control of the project-implementation process is still relatively new, but has already yielded some important implications for project managers and those charged with the successful introduction of IS technology. The information in this chapter provides some guidelines that project managers can employ to more efficiently assign their personnel and resources. It is particularly encouraging to note that the critical factors mentioned in the three studies are all within the control of the IS project manager. These issues are addressable in that remedial action can be taken in the event that problems do occur. Consequently, this chapter not only lists the important CSF, but it also offers advice on their most effective use. It is through employing this *actionable* set of CSF that IS managers and their projects are most likely to benefit.

Feature	Package #1	Package #2	User #1	User #2
Indirect and Direct Billing	+	–/+	5	3
Loss Ratio Reports	–	+	0	5
Report Generator	+	–	1	5
Diary and Activity Log	–	+	4	3
Etc.				

5 denotes absolute *must have*, and 0 indicates *not needed*

Table 4.6   Features

Techniques for Project Selection, Planning, and Scheduling

Nothing in progression can rest on its original plan. We may as well think of rocking a grown man in the cradle of an infant.

Edmund Burke

Sound project selection, planning, scheduling, and control form the cornerstone of any successful implementation effort. These processes have much in common; yet, they are characterized by important distinctions that need to be addressed.

Project selection is the process of critically evaluating multiple project opportunities to ensure that the projects selected for funding are most beneficial to the organization in the long run. Most companies face a visible project backlog of about 2.5 years. In the face of an inability to fund and provide the resources to support all candidate projects, it is necessary to make accurate decisions about which projects should be supported.

Planning is the process of creating a realistic road map that will guide us from the start of our project journey to its intended conclusion. It defines what work must be performed to meet the project objectives and, therefore, also makes evident work that is not a part of the project. Planning includes estimating the time and other resources required to perform each activity.

Planning does not consider when in time an activity is going to be performed, but rather considers only the technological sequence or relationship between activities. Original planning should focus on defining the best way to perform the project. If the resulting plan proves unsatisfactory when scheduled, the necessary changes will become evident, and if a less desirable (e.g., more costly or more risky) plan is required, changes can be made only to those portions of the plan that really help solve the problems.

Scheduling is the process of determining possible times in which each activity can be performed, analyzing resource requirements, and resolving conflicts for resources to arrive at a feasible schedule that is both consistent with technological relationships and resource availability. The schedule informs those responsible for performing activities when they should start and finish. It provides the basis for measuring progress, analyzing problems, and taking corrective action.

Controlling is "the process of comparing actual performance with planned performance, analyzing variances, evaluating possible alternatives, and taking appropriate corrective action as needed" (PMI Standards Committee 1996). This requires a clearly defined and documented plan and a schedule that is feasible, both technically and relative to the resources available to carry out the plan, i.e., the outputs of planning and scheduling. The plan and schedule that are accepted as the basis for comparison comprise the baseline. Approved changes are incorporated to ensure that the project is being performed and progress is being measured against a continuously feasible baseline. Unrealistic expectations can lead to a loss of team morale and overruns in both time and cost.

The common language for planning, scheduling, and controlling projects is the project network diagram (PND). This is a familiar concept to all IS personnel, as it resembles a system or computer-program flowchart. Activities are represented by nodes, and sequence is denoted by arrows. A major difference is that in PNDs, loops are not allowed (at least at the level of sophistication of this discussion). The PND will be discussed in more detail later.

There are a number of useful benefits that can be derived from early and comprehensive planning and scheduling.

- It illustrates in a clear fashion the interrelatedness of all activities in the project.
- It aids in creating a working *team* out of individual members of the implementation staff, as they realize that their responsibilities are interrelated, and that their success can only be consonant with overall project success.
- It provides an informed estimate of the completion date for implementing the IS.

- It minimizes potential departmental conflicts through emphasizing task interrelatedness.
- It improves team members' motivation by providing feedback on individual and group progress against promised milestones.
- It illustrates which tasks must be run in sequence and which may be run in parallel in order to achieve the earliest possible completion date.
- It identifies *critical tasks*, which, if delayed, will delay the installation and adoption of the IS.

There are also useful benefits to be derived from improved control of the project.

- Timely and efficient completion of the project results in a better image and greater respect for the implementation team and each of its members.
- Early recognition of problems permits corrective action when it is relatively economical and painless.
- There is a greater likelihood that resources will be made available when needed, thus avoiding delays and inefficiencies.
- Confidence in the implementation team will result in greater willingness of management to approve future requests for technological improvements for the organization.

Prioritizing Information System Projects

As an IS manager, one of the most important games you may play involves setting priorities for IS project proposals. Although there is no standard accepted technique for ranking IS project proposals, the challenge is clear: Managers must evaluate proposals on a variety of tangible and intangible factors; they must identify and weigh these factors to reflect organizational priorities, and, ideally, the process should be easy to explain and defend, so recommendations are adopted and politics tamed (Millet 1994).

By selecting the best development projects, CIOs can leverage limited resources to the organization's greatest advantage. Furthermore, the ranking process itself can be used to improve communications with user departments and top executives. Unfortunately, most companies rely on methods that leave a great deal to be desired.

One typical problem is lack of attention to intangible benefits and organizational goals. Cost/benefit analyses, for example, focus too much on financial measures. Executives often sense that the analysis is not complete, and so they tend to rely less on the formal process and more on input from other managers and on their own intuition. A CEO of a northeastern United States (U.S.) insurance company, for example, has overturned a steering committee's negative recommendation about a project aimed at better serving insurance agents. Although the cost/benefit analysis was unfavorable, the CEO voted the project in anyway because it fit the business strategy.

Another typical problem is lack of structure. In many organizations, the ranking process is conducted in a fog: Reams of pages and hours of presentations are hashed over by a committee until a prioritized list magically emerges. In these situations, user departments will not understand or trust the process. Similarly, the steering committee will find it difficult to justify and defend its own recommendations.

In this haze of misunderstanding and mistrust, politics thrive. Managers may push for projects catering to their own departments and pet ideas, particularly if development costs are not charged to user departments. Similarly, IS managers may be guilty of promoting large-scale, high-technology projects for the excitement, resources, job security, and résumé enhancement they provide. Executives, meanwhile, may enjoy participating in the game simply to exercise their power and collect IOUs from other managers.

LIMITATIONS OF SCORING TABLES

As a partial remedy to the problems mentioned earlier, many organizations use scoring techniques that combine evaluations on multiple criteria into a final tally. For example, a scale of 1 to 5 may be used to evaluate project proposals on two criteria: 1) financial performance, and, 2) contribution to quality. These may be given weights of 100 and 50 points, respectively, indicating that financial performance is considered twice as important as contribution to quality. A project that scored a 2 on the first criterion and a 4 on the second will receive a weighted total score of $(2 \times 100) + (4 \times 50) = 400$ points.

Although the scoring method addresses the need to impose structure and combine multiple criteria, it suffers from several limitations. On the technical side, it is simply wrong to treat evaluations on this type of scale as real numbers that can be multiplied and summed. If 5 means Excellent, and 4 means Very Good, we know that 5 is better than 4, but we do not know by how much. We cannot even assume that the distance between 5 and 4 is equal to the distance between 4 and 3. This means that if two projects receive scores of 115 and 100 points, respectively, we cannot say that the first project is 15 percent better than the second. Indeed, we cannot even be sure that the first project is better. Many users of scoring models are simply unaware of this technical problem.

Finally, on the managerial side, scoring methodologies provide little support for the selection and weighing of criteria. Frequently, there is no explicit link between the criteria and business objectives. For example, the IS steering committee of a bank may use the criteria of contribution to quality, financial performance, and service. The bank's strategy may focus on customer retention, but these criteria do not recognize this; a project aimed at improving service to potential new customers might score high on service even though it doesn't serve existing customers. Notice also that the criteria of quality and service might overlap, leading to double counting.

THE ANALYTIC HIERARCHY PROCESS

This process, developed by Thomas L. Saaty in the 1970s, addresses technical and managerial problems. Despite some heated debates regarding its theoretical underpinning, this methodology has been used extensively by government and business organizations. Expert Choice Inc. of Pittsburgh (U.S.), the leading vendor of analytic hierarchy process (AHP) software, reports thousands of installations of its namesake product on personal computers around the globe.

Structuring the hierarchy of criteria. The first step in using the AHP is to construct a hierarchy of criteria and subcriteria. The example shown in Figure 5.1 uses financial benefits, contribution to strategy, and contribution to information technology (IT) infrastructure as the main criteria.

The financial benefits criterion, which focuses on tangibles, is divided into short-term and long-term subcriteria. Similarly, contribution to strategy, which focuses on intangibles, is divided into increasing market share for product X, retention of existing customers of product Y, and improving cost management.

The hierarchical structure offers a natural way to divide and conquer the complexities inherent in organizational priorities; without it, managers might simply be overwhelmed. Since the hierarchy can reflect the structure of organizational strategy and critical success factors, it also provides a way to select and justify projects according to their alignment with business objectives.

A large Southern U.S. company used the AHP to rank more than a hundred project proposals worth many millions of dollars. Ten managers from finance, marketing, and management information systems spent a full day just setting the criteria hierarchy. They found that, in addition to clearly defining the evaluative criteria, the process produced a more coherent view of organizational strategy.

Allocating weights to the criteria. The second step in applying the AHP involves allocating a weight to each criterion and splitting that weight among its subcriteria. A pairwise comparison process, in which participants compare each criterion with each of the others one by one,

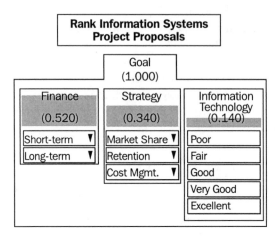

Figure 5.1   Sample Analytical Hierarchy Process Model for Ranking Information System Projects

provides more accurate weights by allowing managers to focus on a series of relatively simple questions.

The sample hierarchy shown in Figure 5.1 indicates that financial benefits received a weight of 52 percent, which is then split 30 percent and 70 percent between its subcriteria. This means that short-term financial benefits receives an overall weight of 52% * 30% = 15.6%.

This hierarchical allocation and splitting of weights addresses the problem of double counting, when listing many similar factors such as quality, service and reputation can result in too much weight being given to what is actually one factor. In the AHP, these factors will be grouped as subcriteria under one criterion and will share its weight.

The weight-allocation process typically produces more insights and can lead to further modifications of the hierarchy. For example, a criterion with marginal importance may be dropped or relegated to a lower level in the hierarchy.

Assigning numerical values to evaluation labels. Once the hierarchy is established, the pairwise comparison process is used again to assign numeric values to the labels that make up the evaluation scale. In Figure 5.1, the five-step scale of Poor, Fair, Good, Very Good, and Excellent was used for each of the bottom criteria. As shown in Figure 5.2, these labels were assigned values of 0, 0.10, 0.30, 0.60, and 1.00, respectively—very different from the naive, equally spaced 1-to-5 scale. In essence, the best evaluation label receives a perfect score of 1.00, and all the other labels receive weights relative to it.

	Nominal	Priority	Bar Graph
Poor	0.00000	0.000	
Fair	0.10000	0.050	
Good	0.30000	0.150	
Very Good	0.60000	0.300	
Excellent	1.00000	0.500	
Total	2.00000	1.000	

Figure 5.2   Assigning Numeric Values to Evaluation Labels

Different scales may be used for each criterion. For example, short-term financial benefits may be evaluated on a scale such as none, less than $50k, $50k to $200k, and more than $200k. The creation of these scales and the allocation of weights within them provide further opportunities to gain insights and drive out ambiguities.

In the Southern U.S. company case, after spending one day on setting up the criteria hierarchy, the team spent an additional full day on allocating weights among the criteria, setting up evaluation scales, and allocating weights within the scales. More recently, one of the authors facilitated the same process for a large insurance firm, and we were able to complete and test the AHP model in just under a day. To support such group processes, Expert Choice has a team version of the AHP software that provides each team member with a remote input device.

Evaluating project proposals. Top-executive input, which is critical in the selection and evaluation of criteria, diminishes once the model is finalized. It is now up to user departments and IS analysts to evaluate project proposals on each of the criteria. Typically, user departments should estimate benefits, while the IS department estimates costs, risks, and contribution to IT infrastructure.

A final score is calculated by multiplying the numeric value of the evaluation the project receives by the weight of the criterion and summing the results across all criteria. In Figure 5.3, results for five projects are displayed. Since Excellent is worth 1.00 point, and Very Good is worth 0.60 points, the Perfect Project, with excellent evaluations on all criteria, scored a total of 1.00, and the All Very Good project scored a 0.60. Both the Aligned and Not Aligned projects received three excellent and three good evaluations; however, the Aligned project scored much higher because its excellent evaluations were on the most important criteria.

Unlike the results of regular scoring models, the distances between AHP scores are significant. The Aligned project, for example, which scored 0.76, is almost three times better than the Mixed project, which

Finance	Short-term

Poor 1 (.000)	Fair 2 (.100)	Good 3 (.300)	Very Good 4 (.600)	Excellent 5 (1.000)

			Finance		Strategy			Technology
	Alternatives	Total	Short-Term	Long-Term	Market Share	Retention	Cost Management	
			.1560	.3640	.1020	.1564	.0816	.1400
1	Perfect Project	1.000	Excellent	Excellent	Excellent	Excellent	Excellent	Excellent
2	Aligned	0.762	Good	Excellent	Good	Excellent	Good	Excellent
3	Not Aligned	0.538	Excellent	Good	Excellent	Good	Excellent	Good
4	All Very Good	0.600	Very Good	Very Good	Very Good	Very Good	Very Good	Very Good
5	Mixed	0.284	Poor	Fair	Good	Very Good	Excellent	Good
6								
7								
8								
9								
10								

Figure 5.3   The Project Rating Spreadsheet

scored only 0.28. This allows us to use the final scores as input to other calculations; for example, we can sort the projects by the ratio of their AHP scores to their implementation costs.

The AHP model can also improve the process of writing and reviewing project proposals. Proposals can be structured to provide self-evaluations, using the criteria of the model. This can drastically reduce information overload on the review committee, and can improve communications and trust among executives, user departments, and IS managers.

Who should take the lead? The current hazy state of affairs may be comfortable and even fun for the IS manager. But, in the long run, the IS manager stands to lose the most from deterioration in communications and trust. IS managers are also under increasing pressure to demonstrate alignment of IT investments with business objectives. The time is ripe, then, for the IS manager to usher in an improved project selection process.

Common Terminology

The following definitions will aid in the discussion of planning, scheduling, and controlling projects.

Scope: "The sum of the products and services to be provided as a project" (PMI Standards Committee 1996; Editor's Note: subsequent quoted material in this section is from the same reference).

Work breakdown structure (WBS): "An organized, hierarchical pre-sentation of the products and services to be provided in a project. The WBS should include the full scope of the project."

Work package: "The lowest level of the WBS. Work packages are composed of multiple activities."

Activity: "An element of work performed during the course of a project. An activity normally has an expected duration plus an expected cost. Activities are often subdivided into tasks."

Project network diagram (PND): "Any schematic display of the logical relationships of project activities. Often incorrectly referred to as a 'PERT chart.'" A PND is often referred to as a critical path method chart, a practice that is somewhat more acceptable.

Path: A sequence of activities defined by the project network logic.

Early start date (ES): "The earliest possible date on which the uncom-pleted portions of an activity (or the project) can start, based on the network logic and any schedule constraints. Early start dates can change as the project progresses and changes are made to the project plan."

Late start date (LS): "The latest possible date that an activity may be begun without delaying a specified milestone (usually the project finish date)."

Float: "The amount of time that an activity may be delayed from its early start without delaying the finish of the project. Float is a mathe-matical calculation and can change as the project progresses and changes are made in the project plan. Also called slack, total float, and path float." In general, float is the difference between the LS date and the ES date (LS – ES).

Critical path: "The path through the project network with the longest duration. The critical path may change from time to time as activities are completed ahead of or behind schedule." Critical path activities have the least amount of float in the project.

Critical path method (CPM): "A network analysis technique used to determine which sequence of activities (which path) has the least amount of scheduling flexibility (the least amount of float) and will thus most likely determine when the project can be completed." It involves the cal-culation of early (forward scheduling) and late (backward scheduling) start and finish dates for each activity. Implicit in this technique is the assumption that whatever resources are required in any given time period will be available.

Resource-limited schedule: "A project schedule whose start and finish dates reflect expected resource availability. The final project schedule should always be resource limited."

Modern project management: "A term used to distinguish the current broad range of project management (scope, cost; time, quality, risk, etc.) from narrower, traditional use that focused on cost and time."

The Application of Modern Project Management

To aid in discussing the application of these concepts, consider a hypothetical IS project. (Other IS projects would involve similar steps.) Let us assume that, through an initial planning and brainstorming session, it has been determined that eleven major steps must be achieved in order to successfully implement the IS (see Table 5.1).

SCOPE MANAGEMENT

The scope statement is the definition of the project. It states the expectations of the client for the product(s) of the project—i.e., the completed implementation. Acceptance criteria define project completion. The scope statement defines the deliverables and the work content required to produce them. Any deliverables or work content not defined in the scope statement is not a part of the project; thus, it becomes the basis for managing the project.

Managing the project includes ensuring that all deliverables agreed to are produced and that deliverables not agreed to are not included. This is an important and difficult aspect of managing a project. For example, it is common for the client, and often a project team member, to conceive of some small change to the project that will "vastly improve the performance of the resulting system." Unfortunately, such small changes often lead to unintended consequences, including surprises, as, somewhere downstream in the project, the system performs differently than expected per the specifications. Not only can such a small change result in "only a couple of days extra work to develop" but in many days of rework to bring the system back to specifications later. An important tool in managing scope is an effective change-management system. Through careful documentation, review and approval, and consistent discipline on the project team, subsequent surprises can be avoided and the probability of successful project completion enhanced.

A proven technique to aid in managing scope is the WBS, such as that shown in Figure 5.4. It subdivides the project into its major elements and each of those into smaller elements. These bottom elements are the work packages. The topmost element is the product of the project, the completed IS implementation. The second level elements are major deliverables, which lead to project completion. For example, the first element is completed when a working paper has been prepared, which will be the

1. Match information system (IS) to organizational tasks and problems.

2. Identify IS user needs.

3. Prepare an informal preliminary proposal to top management (or other decision-makers) for IS acquisition.

4. Seek and hire an IS consultant.

5. Seek staff and departmental support for the IS.

6. Identify the most appropriate location within the organization for the IS.

7. Prepare a formal proposal for IS introduction.

8. Undertake a request for proposals from IS vendors.

9. Conduct a pilot project (or series of pilot projects), using different IS options.

10. Enter a contract for purchase.

11. Adopt and use IS technology.

Table 5.1   Steps in a Hypothetical Information System Implementation Project

basis for discussing user needs in achieving the second element. Every element in the WBS should have a clearly defined deliverable.

A simple way to develop the WBS is as an indented list, such as that shown in Table 5.2. This can be done using a word processor or in most project planning, scheduling, and control software. Simply put the name of the project at the top, and start identifying the major things that have to be done. Insert new items as they are identified. Try to stay at one level until it is reasonably complete, and then focus on one of those elements and add detail under it. Do not be constrained to working on one element at a time though. It is natural for ideas of activities in another area of the project to occur. Record them in the proper place in the list as they occur. Then come back to the one on which you were focusing. As the process slows, go back over each higher-level element to ensure that all subelements have been identified. Then review the entire list to ensure that all elements appear once and only once, and that they are in the most appropriate location in the list. Finally, examine each element to ensure that the deliverable is clearly identified. Note that nothing about

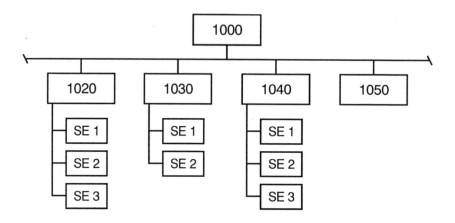

Figure 5.4   Partial Work Breakdown Structure

this process is related to technological precedence, scheduling, or time of occurrence of the element.

After the WBS is, for all practical purposes, completed, add the codes to provide a simple, precise identifier for each element, as shown in the example of Table 5.2.

It is useful at this stage to prepare a work-element dictionary by describing exactly what is expected as the deliverable from each work element. For each element, perform the following steps.

- Develop a statement that shows the necessary inputs, action steps, responsibilities, and expected end results of the activity.
- List any additional organization members who may need to be involved, or whose expertise will need to be tapped.
- Coordinate with cost accounting to establish budget codes and account numbers.
- Identify all relevant resource needs such as additional personnel, computer time, support funds, facilities, equipment, and supplies.

The benefit of using the WBS is that it clearly defines the work that has to be accomplished. If those who will be performing the work in the development of the WBS are involved, they are more likely to *buy in* to the project and resulting system. By using a simple coding system, all members of the project team, as well as the organization's accountants and controllers, will have a common basis for communicating with each other on the progress and status of the implementation. Put together, they provide a full picture of the catalog of activities and milestones that are necessary in order for a geographical information system to be successfully implemented.

Breakdown Code	Description	WBS
	Information System (IS) Installation Project	1000
Element 1	**Match IS to organization tasks and problems.**	**1010**
Subelement 1	Conduct problem analysis.	1011
Subelement 2	Develop information on IS technology.	1012
Subelement 3	Prepare working paper.	1013
Element 2	**Identify IS end users.**	**1020**
Subelement 1	Interview potential users.	1021
Subelement 2	Develop presentation of IS benefits.	1022
Subelement 3	Gain user *buy-in* to the system.	1023
Element 3	**Prepare information proposal.**	**1030**
Subelement 1	Develop cost-benefit information.	1031
Subelement 2	Develop presentation.	1032
Element 4	**Seek and hire consultant.**	**1040**
Subelement 1	Delegate members of search committee.	1041
Subelement 2	Develop selection criteria.	1042
Subelement 3	Interview and select consultants.	1043
Element 5	**Seek staff and departmental support for IS.**	**1050**
Element 6	**Identify the appropriate location for IS.**	**1060**
Subelement 1	Consult with physical plant engineers.	1061
Subelement 2	Identify possible alternative sites.	1062
Subelement 3	Secure site approval.	1063
Element 7	**Prepare formal proposal for IS introduction.**	**1070**

Table 5.2   Work Breakdown Structure for Hypothetical Information System Adoption

Continued on next page

Breakdown Code	Description	WBS
Element 8	**Obtain proposals from vendors.**	**1080**
Subelement 1	Develop request-for-proposal document.	1081
Subelement 2	Contact appropriate vendors.	1082
Subelement 3	Select winner(s) and inform loser(s).	1083
Element 9	**Conduct a pilot project (or series of projects).**	**1090**
Subelement 1	Develop request-for-proposal document.	1091
Element 10	**Contact appropriate vendors.**	**1100**
Subelement 1	Select winner(s) and inform loser(s).	1101
Element 11	**Adopt and use IS technology.**	**1110**
Subelement 1	Initiate employee-training sessions.	1111
Subelement 2	Develop monitoring system for technical problems.	1112

Table 5.2—*Continued*

ESTIMATING

Estimating can now proceed by identifying the resources, durations, and costs for each work package (bottom-level WBS element). In Table 5.3, only the codes for the WBS elements are used, the responsible person has been identified, the duration estimated, and the costs added for each work package. The costs are then, in successive rows, accumulated upward to the next higher work element and finally for the project as a whole. This capability will be especially useful in tracking progress based on estimated cost and actual progress for each activity.

As expenses are incurred, actual costs are tabulated and recorded against the respective activity. The cost recorded can be compared with the costs scheduled to have been incurred to indicate schedule progress. They can be compared with the cost budgeted for work actually accomplished to indicate if spending is on, over, or under budget.

Remember that the key to effective use of the CPM is making judicious and realistic estimates for each activity. It does no good to incorporate a series of *pie-in-the-sky* estimates and milestone schedules that

WBS Code		Responsibility	Duration	Budget
1000		**Bob Williams, IS Manager**		$702,750
1010		Sharon Thomas	14	$7,750
	1011	Sharon Thomas	$2,500	
	1012	Susan Wilson	$2,500	
	1013	Kent Salfi	$2,500	
1020		David LaCouture	4	$2,750
	1021	David LaCouture	$1,000	
	1022	Kent Salfi	$1,000	
	1023	David LaCouture	$750	
1030		James Montgomery	5	$2,000
	1031	James Montgomery	$2,000	
	1032	Bob Williams	$0	
1040		Susan Wilson	4	$2,500
	1041	Sharon Thomas	$0	
	1042	Susan Wilson	$1,500	
	1043	David LaCouture	$1,000	
1050		Susan Wilson	4	$0
1060		Susan Wilson	2	$1,500
	1061	Beth Deyzie	$0	
	1062	David LaCouture	$750	
	1063	Beth Deyzie	$750	
1070		James Montgomery	9	$2,000
1080		Sharon Thomas	3	$250
	1081	Kent Salfi	$0	
	1082	Beth Deyzie	$250	
	1083	Bob Williams	$0	
1090		Sharon Thomas	30	$30,000
1100		Bob Williams	30	$600,000
1110		David LaCouture	90	$54,000
	1111	David LaCouture	$30,000	
	1112	Sharon Thomas	$24,000	

Table 5.3   Cost and Personnel Assignments for Information System Installation

simply cannot be met. Further, that approach can be very damaging, not just to the manager's reputation and the perceived status of the IS by upper management, but also to the morale of the implementation team. For example, consider situations in which the subordinates are given an activity with a time frame that they know to be completely unrealistic. Instead of being motivated to perform the task within that unrealistic schedule, most subordinates are likely to lose motivation and make only minimal attempts to achieve their objectives. The same admonition holds true for the process of developing schedule milestones for a system implementation. Unless the process is given careful consideration, and accurate forecasting and estimation are used, not only will CPM not help, but also it can actually hinder the likelihood of bringing the system online at all.

Note: For simplicity of presentation, the following discussion will focus only on a summary network for level-1 WBS work elements.

In addition to knowing who is primarily responsible for each activity, it is useful to document other responsibilities on the project. This can be done with the activity responsibility matrix (often call a linear responsibility matrix), as shown for the hypothetical project in Table 5.4. In this example, four types of responsibilities are shown: 1) performing the activity, 2) supporting the activity, 3) whom to notify upon completion of the activity, and, 4) from whom approval must be sought prior to beginning the activity.

Activity responsibility matrix. To develop an activity responsibility matrix, list each activity or its code down the left-most column, and list the personnel who have responsibilities for the project across the top. Place the relevant symbol in the pertinent cells to indicate the nature of the responsibilities. This responsibility chart clarifies each person's role and responsibility, relative to each activity.

PROJECT NETWORK DIAGRAM

The next step is to describe the logical relationships between the activities in the project. This is easily done by using the PND, as shown in Figure 5.5.

Draw a rectangle for each activity, place the appropriate code in the rectangles, and connect them with arrows to show the necessary sequence. Avoid considering anything but technological requirements at this stage. For example, activities 1010 (match IS to organizational tasks and problems) and 1020 (identify IS user needs) can proceed in parallel, but both need to be completed prior to 1030 (preparing the informal proposal). After 1030 is completed, activities 1040, 1050, and 1060 can proceed in parallel leading into 1070. Activity 1080 proceeds after the proposal is approved, followed by 1090, then 1100, and then 1110.

WBS Element	WBS Element Managers				
	Bob	Sharon	David	James	Susan
1010	N	R	—	—	S
1020	N	—	R	N	—
1030	@	—	—	R	—
1040	@	S	S	—	R
1050	S	—	N	S	R
1060	—	—	—	—	R
1070	@	S	—	R	—
1080	S	R	—	—	—
1090	N	R	—	—	S
1100	R	—	N	—	—
1110	—	S	R	—	—

Legend:

R = Responsible   S = Support   N = Notification   @ = Approval

Table 5.4   Activity Responsibility Matrix

CRITICAL PATH METHOD CALCULATIONS

Having developed the PND, the next step is to calculate the early and late start and finish dates. This is presented in Table 5.5. The dates are represented as day numbers and denote the beginning of the respective day.

Very briefly, the calculation of early starts and finishes (as in forward scheduling) is as follows.

■ Activities 1010 and 1020 have no predecessors and are therefore beginning activities. They can start at time zero (0). Their duration is 14 and 4 days, thus the earliest they can finish is time 14 and 4.

■ Activity 1030 is preceded by 1010 and 1020. The earliest that both of these can be finished is 14; therefore, the earliest that 1030 can start is 14. Having a duration of 5, 1030 has an early finish of 19.

■ Activities 1040, 1050, and 1060 cannot start until 1030 is finished, i.e., time 19; they can finish at times 23, 23, and 21.

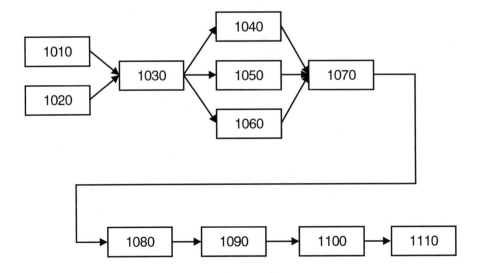

Figure 5.5   Project Network Diagram for Hypothetical Project

■ Activity 1070, being dependent on the above three, cannot start until all of them are completed, i.e., time 23, and therefore can finish no earlier than 32.

■ Activity 1080 cannot start until 1070 is finished, time 32, and therefore can finish no earlier than time 35.

■ Activities 1090, 1100, and 1110 follow in sequence, with each starting when its predecessor is completed.

■ The project is not finished until all activities in the project are completed. The latest early finish for all activities in the project is therefore time 185; thus, the earliest the project can be finished is time 185.

The calculation of the latest start and finish times (as in backward scheduling) are as follows.

■ In backward scheduling, the ending activity is assigned a latest finish time. The ending activity in this example is clear, due to the simplicity of the project and the order of listing of the activities. A more general rule to identify ending activities is that they are not shown as the predecessor of any other activity. Consider each activity, one at a time. Scan the predecessor column for the occurrence of that activity. All will be found, with the exception of 1110, which is therefore an ending activity. It could be assigned any finish time for calculation purposes. The earliest project completion time was chosen for simplicity and clarity of presentation of the comparison between earliest and latest times.

■ Activity 1110 has a duration of 90 days. Therefore, it must start no later than time 95, or it will delay the completion of the project. It is preceded by activity 1100, which must be completed by no later than 95 if 1110 is to be started at 95.

■ Activity 1100 must be finished no later than time 95; therefore, it must start no later than time 65 in order to finish at time 95.

■ Activity 1090 must start no later than time 35 to finish by time 65, and activity 1080 must start no later than time 32.

■ Similarly, 1070 must be started at time 23 to avoid delaying project completion. Its predecessors—1040, 1050, and 1060—must all be finished no later than time 23, or 1070 or the project will be delayed.

■ The calculations proceed back to 1030, which has two predecessors, 1010 and 1020. They both must be completed by time 14 to avoid delaying the project.

■ The beginning activities, 1010 and 1020, must therefore be started no later than times 0 and 10, respectively.

FLOAT

Total float is simply the difference between the time available and the time required to perform an activity. For example, activity 1010 can start at time 0 and must be finished by time 14, giving a time available of 14 days. It requires 14 days to perform, giving it 0 (zero) total float. Similarly, 1020 can start at 0 and must be finished no later than 14, again a time available of 14 days as compared to a required duration of 4 days. Thus, it has 10 days of total float. For the level of analysis presented here, it is convenient to recognize that total float is equal to late start minus early start, or late finish minus early finish.

Two activities have positive total float, 1020 and 1060. They are not critical; i.e., they can be delayed from their earliest starts without delaying project completion. The activities with 0 (zero) total float are critical.

Careful examination indicates that there are two critical paths in this project, as it is currently planned. They must be monitored carefully to minimize the chances of any of these activities *slipping*, for that could delay completion of the project.

Take note that no consideration has been given to resources required or available to this point. Thus, if resources are limited, the project may require more than 185 days for completion.

Three activities in Table 5.5 are marked with asterisks to indicate that they are milestones. That is, they are key decision or action dates. They are important as intermediate points; management should monitor them

Activities	Predecessors	Duration	Early Start	Early Finish	Late Start	Late Finish	Total Float
1010	—	14	0	14	0	14	0
1020	—	4	0	4	10	14	10
1030*	1010 1020	5	14	19	14	19	0
1040	1030	4	19	23	19	23	0
1050	1030	4	19	23	19	23	0
1060	1030	2	19	21	21	23	0
1070*	1040 1050 1060	9	23	32	23	32	2
1080	1070	3	32	35	32	35	0
1090	1080	30	35	65	35	65	0
1100*	1090	30	65	95	65	95	0
1110	1100	90	95	185	95	185	0

*Milestone

Table 5.5   Early and Late Calculations for Hypothetical Project

for early warning of potential problems. The importance of these milestones is discussed later.

GANTT CHARTS

One of the oldest and still most useful tools for communications and analysis is the Gantt chart, as shown in Figure 5.6. It is especially useful in portraying the planned schedule and actual progress. It is easy to read and provides project visibility to both team members and upper management. Very simply, the horizontal axis is calendar time, and the vertical axis shows the individual activities. A bar shows the scheduled start and finish times for the activity. Note activity 1020 is shown to start at time 0 and finish at time 4, showing float of 10 days, exactly as shown in the calculations above.

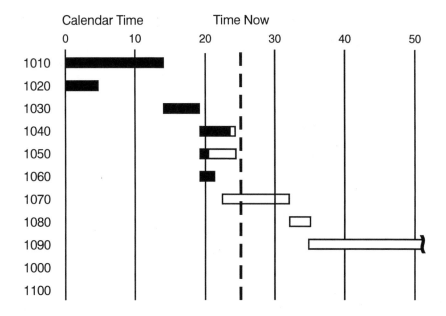

Figure 5.6   Partial Gantt Chart

A common practice is to show only the outline of the activity, as illustrated in Figure 5.6, filling it in to indicate progress. Float, if it is present, is generally indicated by a dashed or dotted extension to the bar, as it is in Figure 5.6. A vertical line at the most recent reporting date is labeled Time Now in Figure 5.6. Activities that are shaded in up to Time Now are on schedule. Those that go past Time Now are ahead of schedule, and those for which the shading does not reach the Time Now line are behind schedule. Anyone—especially the manager charged with the IS implementation—can see at a glance if there are any discrepancies between actual and planned activity start or completion times. When such problems do occur, managers should go back to their computer software to analyze possible alternative reassignment or reallocation of resources and, if necessary, revise the plan.

There are some important advantages in using Gantt charts. First, they are easy to read and interpret. Although they contain a great deal of information, the manner in which they are laid out makes them highly accessible to those who need to determine the status of the implementation at any point in time. Note, however, that a particular Gantt chart is useful until there are major changes to activity schedules or resource reallocations. Once either of these adjustments occurs, the chart must be redrawn.

The Gantt chart is also important to analyze resource requirements by time period. This is especially easy when using a computer program for project planning, scheduling, and controlling.

Note that the CPM and Gantt-chart methodologies are not competing concepts; rather, these tools are most effective when used in combination. The CPM—because it is based on a PND, details the activities that must be finished to complete the project and the sequence in which they can be performed—shows the work that can proceed in parallel (provided the resources are available), and presents the total float as a measure of the flexibility available in scheduling. The Gantt chart is easy to understand because it clearly indicates progress (by shading in the bar), showing if activities are on time, early, or late and, in some versions, can indicate the impact of late performance of one activity on the start of other activities. Used in tandem, the CPM and Gantt Chart provide a set of powerful and readily applicable techniques for implementation scheduling and control.

RESOURCE ANALYSIS

The CPM assumes that whatever resources are required in a time period will be available. Resource analysis goes beyond this assumption to analyze the indicated requirements and compare them against actual availability. Some programs can automatically schedule the project, taking into consideration the resource constraints. Referring to Table 5.3, it can be observed that Susan Wilson is responsible for activities 1040, 1050, and 1060. Table 5.5, as well as Figure 5.6, show that these three activities are to be performed between days 19 and 23. If each takes the full-time attention of Susan, she will be grossly overworked in that time period. She is likely to fail to complete all of these tasks in the time available and, thus, likely to delay the project.

One alternative is to assign another individual responsibility for one or more activities. Another is to replan the project to avoid this conflict. Still another alternative is to delay the completion of the project by six days.

A feasible schedule is determined after analyzing all the resources for such conflicts and resolving those that are found. The results of this process must be carefully analyzed to ensure that nothing was overlooked. Afterward, the schedule can be published for review by the project team, and then by upper management.

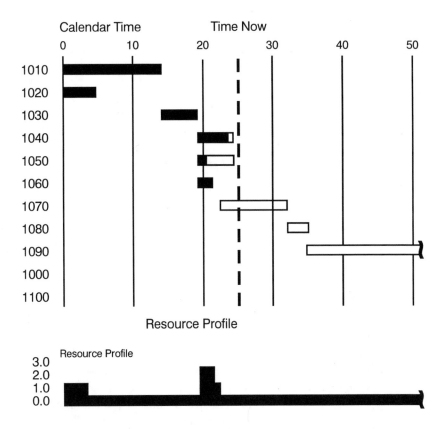

Figure 5.7   Resource Analysis Histogram

MANAGEMENT REVIEW

Having completed the planning and scheduling processes, there should be a review by upper management, as well as by all the personnel who will be assigned responsibility for ensuring that the work of each of these activities is performed. This step is important because it accomplishes two objectives. First, it helps to determine whether the projections are accurate and achievable. Is the IS manager who made the preliminary assignments operating under full information, or are there additional issues and constraints of which this individual is not aware? Second, the review aids in creating buy-in of the entire plan on the part of the personnel selected to perform these tasks. Gaining their approval and possible suggestions for the plan's improvement go a long way toward ensuring that they are confident in the planning that has been done, and are committed to fulfilling the objectives of their specific activities.

In fact, to the extent possible, it is desirable to have periodic review meetings with those who will be a part of the project team, as the planning and scheduling processes proceed. Their involvement at early stages will contribute even more to their buy-in.

CONTROLLING

Controlling is not going around with a *big stick*, prodding everyone to work harder. It is keeping well informed as to actual progress and taking any action that is warranted to remove obstacles, counsel with team members who are having difficulty, and providing incentives to complete their activities according to schedule. The most difficult part of this process may well be to conduct regular progress reviews with the individuals involved, as well as with the entire team. The pressure to produce results will detract from the conduct of such reviews unless strong personal discipline is exercised.

NORMATIVE VERSUS ACTUAL PLANNING AND SCHEDULING

You may have wondered how anyone could put together a plan and schedule of any magnitude as accurately as described in the earlier discussion. Actually, to simplify the presentation, we have presented the *normative* view—i.e., how you ought to do it in an ideal world. The actual planning and scheduling processes may well require several iterations, especially at each milestone. For example, one iteration might be accurate up to the *informal proposal* stage. That version may very well be somewhat abbreviated, showing the detailed activities only up to the informal proposal completion. It is likely that an update will be made prior to the presentation of this informal presentation and another after, if there are any changes in direction. That plan and schedule will probably suffice until the formal proposal is prepared. Again, there will likely be two iterations at this point. The next milestone is signing the contract. New information becomes available from the vendor that again requires updating the plan and schedule.

At each step in this process, a comparison against the original and most recently approved baselines will provide an audit trail of the changes. The successive iterations and the comparisons are major reasons for using a computer-based planning, scheduling, and control software package. There are a variety of these on the market, and the one chosen should provide capabilities commensurate with the needs of the organization and the projects to which it will be applied.

MANAGING THE CHANGE CONTROL PROCESS

It has long been recognized that software configuration management is a key requirement for maintaining successful control of the project (Paulk, Curtis et al. 1993; Paulk, Weber et al. 1993). One of the most problematic areas within software configuration management is change control; how do we handle the seemingly endless stream of requests for changes to the system? These requests can come not only from the user community, but also from the developers themselves:

> What was supposed to be a midyear release for the next version of Penpoint—which was to occupy substantially less memory and be much easier to use—began to slide inexorably toward the dead of winter. Most of the engineers were occupied with simplifying portions of the program to reduce its size. But in the course of rewriting, everyone was proposing improvements that would tend to increase its size. Penpoint was succumbing to a disease called feature creep— the irresistible temptation for engineers to load a product down with their favorite special features. Before unnecessary additions hardened around their feet like concrete, the senior technical managers staged meetings called Feature Court, with "Judge Wapner" presiding. Each side would argue its case, and a binding decision was made on the spot. Despite these efforts, the system seemed to grow like a cancer. No sooner were we able to save some space than a new, indispensable requirement would emerge. (*Fortune* 29 May 1995)

Change control aims at directing all change requests through a centralized triage process. Some requests get rejected, some get delayed to the next version, and some are approved for current version implementation in a manner that maintains the integrity of the system.

The next-version problem. On paper this sounds great, but in reality politics, uncertainty, and doubt play havoc with the change control process. Things tend to get particularly nasty when users find their change requests thrown onto the next-version pile by the triage process. Users can typically understand the justification for the *no* decisions, but tell seasoned users that their enhancement request is a good idea, yet it will have to wait for the next version, and they will assume your fingers are crossed behind your back.

Most users know that when the first version of the project gets completed, the developers will probably be assigned to higher priority projects. Hence, the next version may never happen. It is no surprise then that users react to the uncertainty of the next-version promise with doubt. This leads to tremendous pressure for squeezing every viable enhancement idea into the current version. Each of these changes propagates as a disruptive wave throughout the implementation process, and the project gets stuck in a dysfunctional zone of constant change with very little progress.

Solutions. Here are a few things you can do to mitigate these pressures. First, there is the obvious step of providing management with time and cost-impact assessments. If the users insist on having certain changes squeezed into the current version, ask top management to approve the necessary delays and additional resources. The potential for inflating these estimates raises some interesting ethical questions, but that is a topic for another book.

The problem with the impact-assessment approach is that it raises a conflict between you, as project manager, and the user community, to the attention of top management. You should prefer dissolving this conflict directly with the users, rather than resolving it with top-management intervention.

The key to resolving this conflict is to convince users that the organization is serious about the next version. The necessary steps may cost you only a few dollars, and we have seen them used with great success.

Start by purchasing a large three-ring binder, one that has a wide enough spine to accommodate a title, such as Version 2.0 (or even better, Version 1.1), displayed in large letters. This is where all next-version triage memos should be filed. This folder should be prominently displayed in the project manager's office and should be dragged into every meeting with users. A current list of items in that folder may also be managed on a Web site.

Next, appoint someone on your project staff to the position of Version 2.0 Manager. This person should probably be one of the senior systems analysts who participates in the change-control review process and is known and liked by the user community. Announce this new appointment in a manner that cannot escape the attention of the user community. This analyst may be so flattered by the new title that he may forget to ask for a pay raise.

At this point, the duties of this new manager may be limited to filing the appropriate triage memos in the new binder and participating in a few more meetings. In those cases when a change request is assigned to the next version, the user should be informed of the item number under which it has been filed in the Version 2.0 binder. In certain cases, the feedback memo to the user should be supplemented with a phone call or a meeting to explain the rationale for the decision.

The objective is to turn the abstract notion of the next version into a concrete and visible one. The binder and the manager title cost you very little, and they provide the user community with the sense that the next version is something indeed planned to undertake, and that requests that were approved for the next version are being carefully tracked.

Finally, for projects where you expect requests from many users, you should divide the user community into organizational or functional groups, and request that each group select a single person to act as a liaison for the project. These liaisons quickly develop a better understanding of project issues and, hence, can better understand and convey the rationale for the decisions made during the change-control process. They can also do a better job of communicating requests to the project team.

Note: Assigning users to project liaison positions is an extremely useful technique that provides benefits far beyond the contribution to the change-control process.

Conclusions

The usefulness of these techniques to IS implementation managers is only good if they are used. This chapter provides the basic outlines of these planning, scheduling, and control tools. Any manager who wishes to do so should read about these procedures thoroughly. For that purpose, a list of recommended readings on planning, scheduling, and controlling is included at the back of the book. These bibliographic selections offer more in-depth discussion of these techniques, often with sample problems for practice. Some managers may find it useful to take courses in project management techniques in order to gain additional mastery of this topic. Lists of training opportunities are published by the Project Management Institute in its *PM Network* magazine.

The Politics of Implementation

Politics is the conduct of public affairs for private advantage.

Ambrose Bierce

The Setup

Two minutes ago you were ushered into the office of the CIO. Your heart is going turbo upon hearing that you have been handpicked to head a new system development project. The CIO asks you if you think you can handle this wonderful challenge and bring the project to completion on time and within budget.

What should you do now? You are happy, proud, and flattered. Your first instinct may be to thank the CIO and provide assurance that you can handle this challenge, and that you will do your best to make this project a success. If you do that, you may find yourself in the corridor within two more minutes with the responsibility of delivering on your promise, or failing—probably, you'll fail.

Avoiding the Sting

There is no reason to hide your feelings. Feel free to express how happy, proud, and flattered you are. However, do not accept the assignment yet.

Ask for a second meeting at a later date, allowing you sufficient time to investigate the project requirements, resources, and schedule constraints. Even if the CIO tells you that these issues can always be resolved later, refuse to immediately accept the assignment.

You should accept responsibility for a project only after being convinced that you have a fair chance of succeeding. This sounds obvious, but we have seen many cases when systems professionals accepted responsibility for doomed projects.

The first thing you should check is the justification for the project. If you are not convinced that the project is justified, then, for ethical as well as pragmatic reasons, you should stay clear of it. Next you should investigate the level of support for the project among users and other stakeholders. While a certain level of resistance is unavoidable, you should avoid projects that are doomed to failure due to organizational resistance, or because the necessary approval processes were circumvented.

Once you are convinced that the project is viable, you must assess the resources and schedule constraints to which you will commit; if you think they are not reasonable, negotiate for changes. This negotiation can take place at the second meeting or, even better, it can begin with a short but well-supported memo.

You may fear that, by acting this way, you will come across as hesitant, uncooperative, and fearful of responsibility. If, however, you handle the review and negotiation process in a professional manner that revolves around a clear project assessment and execution plan, you will actually come across as smart, resourceful, and dependable.

This is only one small example of how political awareness can save your career. The message is: Politics matters. You should care about politics, even if you do not care for politics.

The Problem with Politics

Few topics generate as much heat and as many passionate feelings as a discussion of political behavior. Most organizational personnel are quick to condemn politics and their chief practitioners—company *politicians*—as predatory and counter to the interests of the overall organization. In fact, it is unlikely to find individuals with even minimal organizational experience who have not had some bad experiences with office politics in their careers. Nevertheless, surprisingly little is known about organizational politics and its true impact on individuals within organizations.

One of the areas where politics is better understood—particularly its impact—is in the process of implementing innovations such as new information systems (IS) in organizations. Anecdotal and case-study information abound, which strongly reinforce the importance of understanding and effectively utilizing organizational politics as a tool in successful IS implementation. Without an understanding of the role that politics plays in IS implementation, the likelihood of successfully managing the adoption of an IS will be significantly diminished.

The purpose of this chapter is to explore, in some detail, the concept of organizational politics, developing some of the well-acknowledged themes that pervade the topic. To gain an understanding of the role that politics plays in the successful implementation of IS, it is important to examine the various definitions of politics that are usually employed. No matter which definition of politics is used, the end result is the same: Political behavior is a method for dealing with basic organizational conflicts. Unfortunately, although often used as a method for resolving conflicts, the irony is that political behavior itself usually becomes a contributing cause of additional organizational conflict. Finally, some suggestions are offered to project managers on how to effectively operate within the political arena of organizations, not to achieve predatory and self-serving ends but in an effort to smooth the process by which their systems are adopted.

What Is Organization Politics?

Probably no topic has generated as much heat and general disagreement as the notion of corporate politics. Writers and researchers usually find that they cannot even agree on a uniform definition of politics, let alone acknowledge the role of politics in organizational life. When one sifts through the information on power and politics, a number of definitions are suggested, often with varying degrees of usefulness.

THE NEGATIVE VIEW OF POLITICS

Among the definitions of politics, some important patterns can be discerned and help in establishing a framework for understanding the concept. For example, one colleague has referred to politics as self-interested behavior with guile. Another definition suggests that politics involves "those activities taken within an organization to acquire, develop, and use power to get one's way" (Pfeffer 1981, 7). Henry Mintzberg, another well-known researcher in organization theory, suggests that politics encompasses modern organizations, referring to organizations as "system(s) captured by conflict" (1983, 421). Yet another definition of politics offers the characterization that political behavior is inherently competitive and focused on satisfying self-interests (Mayes and Allen 1977, 675). These and other definitions of the *negative school* generally characterize political behavior as essentially malevolent, conflict laden, self-aggrandizing, and unhealthy. The basic attitude can be summarized by the following arguments about the nature of politics.

Behavior designed to benefit the individual or group at the organization's expense. This idea suggests that political behavior is entirely self-serving, predicated on getting ahead in spite of the possible side effects to the organization as a whole. For example, managers who actively pursue personal agendas—advancing their own positions in the company in any way possible—may think nothing of continually withholding information that could make them look bad, even if that information is vital to the top-management team for strategic decision-making. For example, over a decade ago, a researcher engaged in a long-term study of steel-mill operations within a Fortune 500 steel company. After spending over twelve months collecting data, the researcher was forced to abandon the study when he discovered that the mills routinely falsified productivity reports, thereby influencing top management to make poor strategic decisions based on flawed data. The managers were more concerned with maintaining their own power bases through political maneuvering than in seeking ways to best aid the company.

The displacement of legitimate power. *Legitimate* power is defined as the power that accrues to an individual due to her position within the organization (French and Raven 1959). For example, bosses who simply rely on the position they occupy as a basis for giving orders are said to make use of legitimate power. Politics has the capacity to displace legitimate power through maneuvers designed to circumvent the legitimate authority structure of the organization. For example, consider a situation in which a three-person chain of command exists: Sue is at the top, Bob is her subordinate, and Allen is Bob's subordinate. Allen would be exercising a political approach if he habitually found ways to *end-run* Bob's authority by going directly to Sue to mediate disagreements, solve problems, or offer advice. Allen could pick any of a number of ways to cultivate Sue's help from joining the same civic organizations, church, country club, and so on in an effort to create a personal relationship with Sue. Allen is banking on this relationship as a bulwark against Bob being able to use his legitimate authority. Allen has attempted to displace Bob's authority through political behavior.

The use of means not sanctioned by the organization to attain sanctioned ends, or the use of sanctioned means to obtain unsanctioned ends. This proposition has two elements. First, it suggests that political behavior might actually be used in the interests of the organization. Unfortunately, this behavior would be widely perceived as unethical or immoral. Recently, for example, the chairman and CEO of Bath Iron Works, a major shipbuilding company with extensive defense department contracts, resigned in disgrace following the disclosure that he had illegally accepted and made use of photocopied Department of Defense documents of a sensitive and secret nature. These documents gave his firm an unfair advantage in bidding for new contracts. Obviously, it was in the interest of his company to win those contracts. Equally obvious, however, he violated the law (using unsanctioned means) in gaining this competitive advantage and, following his resignation, his company was forced to pay a substantial fine for his actions.

The second aspect of this proposition suggests that political behavior may involve using acceptable means to obtain unacceptable ends. Again, the issue has to do with the degree to which political actors are willing to bend moral or ethical codes to gain an advantage. There are many actions in which an individual or organization can engage that are legal, but may be highly questionable from an ethical perspective. To illustrate, Johns-Manville Corporation received a great deal of bad press some years ago when, following the ban on the use of asbestos in the United States, it began selling its stockpiles overseas to countries that did not have comprehensive health and welfare policies. Note that in this example Johns-Manville did not break the law per se in selling asbestos. On the other hand, knowing that this material was unhealthy (since 1900, Manville had commissioned three internal health studies, all pointing to the same conclusion), it could be argued that the more appropriate course was to acknowledge the health risk and simply destroy the asbestos stocks.

Note that the underlying commonalty among each of the arguments listed above is the notion that political behavior is, at its core, unhealthy, counter to organizational goals, and essentially predatory. Writers who have taken this view have argued, with some heat, that the sooner politics is removed from the organizational arena, the better organizations will be in terms of their operations and personal relationships.

THE NEUTRAL VIEW OF POLITICS

In more recent years, another school of thought has developed to counter the negative school. This second system of thought on organizational politics—while not denying the potential for abusing the use of politics through self-serving behavior and subsequently damaging organizational relationships—tends to take a more neutral view of the process. Its proponents argue that politics and political activity are simply a natural part of organizations, and must be acknowledged as no different, in essence, than a firm's culture or organizational structure. This argument suggests that politics can be characterized as neither good nor bad but as natural and, as such, counters previous arguments by suggesting that efforts or calls to eliminate politics are naive. Politics, this school of thought contends, "exists" and must be learned and applied, preferably in a nonpredatory manner (Allen et al. 1979, 78; Beeman and Sharkey 1987; Markus 1983).

There are five propositions that underscore the neutral, or natural, view of organizational politics. These propositions follow a logical sequencing as they develop the argument for understanding the true nature of politics.

Proposition 1: Most important decisions in organizations involve the allocation of scarce resources. This statement lays the groundwork upon which the context for decision-making is established. When decisions need to be made, particularly in the context of group decisions, they are often triggered by some problem or concern. For example, suppose that the operations of an organization's planning department are fragmented and haphazard. A committee would be charged with devising ways of reworking operating policies or finding alternatives for how operations are conducted. The decision at which it arrives and indeed the decision process itself are almost always bounded by a number of contingency factors. For example, a short time frame for making the recommendations, a limited operating budget, or the concerns and prerogatives of senior managers may all form a boundary around which the decision must be made. One of the most compelling boundaries is the notion of scarce resources. Given the limited resources with which to carry out tasks, there are only so many good jobs to go around; there is only so much money that can be spent. The list of constraints is endless. Consequently, any attempts made to arrive at the optimal decision in dealing with a perceived problem are necessarily constrained by the limits of scarce resources.

Not only are most decisions constrained by scarce resources, but also the majority of important decisions made within organizations involve, to one degree or another, the allocation or distribution of these scarce resources among a number of competing demands. Departmental budgets are submitted in order to divide organizational resources in as equitable a manner as possible (at least, in the senior manager's eyes). The decision of whether or not to acquire and install an IS involves the implicit tradeoff between the purchase of that system and other demands that could be met through the money that was budgeted to acquire the IS. Consequently, these points give credence to the argument that decision-making (particularly for important decisions) is in some way bound to the prioritization and distribution of organizational resources.

Proposition 2: The decision process often involves bargaining, negotiating, and jockeying for position. It is likely to come as no surprise to the majority of readers, particularly those who are currently employed in organizations, that the manner in which many decisions are made is often based less on purely logical decision processes than on a variety of intervening criteria. Certainly, as March and Simon noted nearly thirty-five years ago, individuals strive for logic in their decision processes (1958).

However, for a variety of reasons, we are often more likely to be influenced by and make use of a variety of extra or additional criteria in arriving at decision choices (March and Simon 1958). One process, common within organizations where scarce resources are the rule, is to make use of bargaining or negotiating behavior. Bargaining follows one of the most common approaches to dealing with conditions of scarce resources: Individuals and department heads make deals or compromises among the variety of competing desires and organizational reality. Since all parties cannot, by definition, attain everything they seek (due to scarce resources), in order to gain as much advantage as possible, individuals who may be in competitive relationships are forced to compromise or negotiate to gain as much as possible.

Proposition 3: Organizations are coalitions composed of a variety of self-interested groups. It is important to understand that when we refer to an organization, it may be a convenient shortcut to use the term in a monolithic sense. We sometimes believe that an organization can and will act as a single, purposeful entity. In reality, the term *organization* gives meaning to the reality behind this misperception. In both the public and private arenas, organizations are composed of a variety of groups: labor versus management, finance versus marketing, and so forth. These groups, which must be viewed as essentially self-interested, comprise the sum total of an organization. This proposition will, on the surface, raise some objections. For example, the notion that these groups are basically self-interested implies that they are willing to put their own concerns before the legitimate goals and concerns of the organization. Some may object to this characterization, as it implies that these groups will seek their own goals at the expense of what is best for the organization as a whole. In reality, although the different interest groups in the organization generally do buy in to the overall corporate goals, they do so to varying degrees, and rarely are they willing to embrace all of the firm's objectives. The reasons for the reluctance to totally subordinate one's own goals for corporatewide objectives can be understood after reading a discussion of Proposition 4.

Proposition 4: Groups differ in terms of goals, values, attitudes, time frames, and so on. In 1967, a landmark study sought to investigate the manner in which roles and attitudes differ among various subgroups in organizations (Lawrence and Lorsch 1967; Lawrence and Lorsch 1969). Through their research, Lawrence and Lorsch uncovered and introduced a phenomenon that they referred to as "organizational differentiation." The concept of differentiation was used to describe the fact that as individuals enter the organization by joining a functional group such as accounting or marketing, they develop a set of values and goals that are in accord with that functional group. They begin to embrace subgroup values and attitudes instead of strictly organizationwide goals. The reasons for this phenomenon are obvious: It is in their functional reference group (marketing, finance, R&D, and so forth) that individuals are assigned positions, given tasks to perform, evaluated, and rewarded. Hence, their allegiance becomes focused upon their immediate work group.

The second important finding of Lawrence and Lorsch was that these functional groups usually differ in terms of a number of important criteria, including goals, time frames, values, and so on (1967). To illustrate, consider the situation that is often found in organizations having separate R&D and marketing departments. Today, marketing is primarily concerned with making sales to customers. The reward systems (bonuses, promotions, and incentives) for those who work in marketing departments are usually geared toward sales volume achieved. Given reward systems that value sales volume, it is easy to understand the emphasis that marketing personnel place on short-term profitability and *making their numbers*. Compare this value system to that of a typical R&D department, where incentives are related to creativity, innovation, and technological development. These activities cannot be regulated in any way that is similar to the approaches used in marketing. Further, the time frames of R&D personnel are often more long term, aimed at achieving technological development, regardless of how long that may take. Naturally, the short-term, sales-volume goals of marketing not only differ from R&D's long-term focus, but also often actually conflict. In order for marketing personnel to achieve their goals, members of R&D may have to sacrifice theirs.

Here in a nutshell is the basic contradiction uncovered by Lawrence and Lorsch that pervades most organizations. Subgroups within organizations contrast, due to differences in a variety of criteria: time frames, goals, attitudes, values, and so forth. The result of this change in goal criteria is why these groups must to some degree be characterized as self-interested. They feel most keenly the need to achieve their own departmental goals first or, more benevolently, what they believe to be the best interests of the organization, from their unique points of view. These differences are important, because they shape the types of dynamics that almost always characterize the modern organization. These dynamics can be best described by the final proposition.

Proposition 5: Because of scarce resources and enduring differences, power and conflict are central to organizational life. This proposition forms the underlying rationale behind the political model of organizational life. Because of the essential differences and contradictions that exist within organizations, conflict is not simply a side effect of organizational members' interaction; it is a natural and self-perpetuating state. Likewise, political behavior cannot be characterized as malevolent and deviant, but must be seen as a natural consequence of the interaction between organizational subsystems. This *natural* view of politics refuses to condemn the use of political tactics among organizational members, as it views these behaviors as an expected side effect of company life.

Using Politics in Corporations

In presenting both the negative and natural sides of the debate on the nature of corporate politics, it is important to point out that readers need to come to their own conclusions about the role of politics in organizational life. There are usually three distinct positions regarding political behavior taken by individuals as they enter organizational service for the first time; two of these positions are equally inappropriate but for entirely different reasons.

THE NAIVE

The first approach can be best termed the *naive* attitude regarding politics. Naive individuals view politics as unappealing at the outset, and make a firm resolution never to engage in any type of behavior that could resemble political activity. Their goal is, in effect, to remain above the fray, not allowing politics in any form to influence their conduct.

THE SHARK

The second and exact opposite approach is undertaken by individuals who enter organizations with the express purpose of using politics and aggressive manipulation to reach the top. While actually few in number, this type readily embraces political behavior in its most virulent form. Their loyalties are tied entirely to themselves and their own objectives. Try to work with them, and one is likely to be used and manipulated; get between them and their goal, and their behavior may become utterly amoral. While taking care to publicly use the correct words concerning *working for the good of the company* and *developing personal loyalty*, in reality, the only cause these individuals espouse is their own.

POLITICALLY SENSIBLE

Both the naive and the shark are wrong-minded about politics—but for completely different reasons. Their attitudes underscore the awareness of the third type of organizational actor: the *politically sensible*. Figure 6.1 illustrates the differences in attitudes among these three political approaches.

Politically sensible individuals enter organizations with few illusions about how decisions are made. They understand, either intuitively or through their own past experiences and mistakes, that politics is simply

Characteristics	Naive	Sensible	Shark
Underlying Attitude "Politics is ... "	Unpleasant	Necessary	An Opportunity
Intent	Avoid at all costs.	Used to Further Department's Goals	Self-Serving and Predatory
Techniques	"Tell it like it is."	Network, expand connections, use system to give and receive favors.	Manipulation; Use of Fraud and Deceit When Necessary

Figure 6.1   Characteristics of Political Behaviors

another side, albeit sometimes an unattractive one, of the behavior in which one must engage in order to succeed in modern organizations. While not shunning politics, neither do they embrace its use. Instead, the politically sensible are apt to state that this behavior is at times necessary because "that is the way the game is played." It is also important to note that politically sensible individuals generally do not play politics of a predatory nature, as do sharks who are seeking to advance their own careers in any manner that is expedient. Politically sensible individuals use politics as a way of making contacts, cutting deals, and gaining power and resources for their departments in order to further corporate, rather than entirely personal, ends.

THE PRAGMATIC CHOICE

Everyone must make up his own mind regarding the efficacy and morality of engaging in corporate politics. Interviews of successful managers would show that it is almost impossible to be successful in organizational systems without a basic understanding of and willingness to employ organizational politics. Whatever position one adopts, research on the topic has led to some important conclusions about politics. A recent large-scale study of senior and mid-level managers offered a number of interesting conclusions about the use of politics in organizations (Gandz and Murray 1980):

- While unable to agree whether or not politics is a natural process, most managers regard politics in a negative manner and view political behavior as unprofitably consuming organizational time and resources.
- Managers believe that political behavior is common to all organizations.
- The majority of managers believes that political behavior is more prevalent among upper managers than among those at lower levels in organizations.
- Political behavior is much more common in certain decision domains, such as structural change or new system implementation, than in other types of organizational activities, such as handling employee grievances.

The fourth conclusion is particularly relevant to our discussion of politics. The reason why political behavior is more common under certain conditions such as new system introduction is that these types of organizational changes signal the potential for a significant shift in power relationships. Any form of organizational change has the potential to alter the power landscape because one important determinant of power is the notion of centrality (Hickson et al. 1971). Centrality refers to how central to the main activities of an organization a particular individual or department operates. The more central the department's activities are to the organization's mission, the greater the power held by that department. The implementation of a new IS has the potential to remove the power of centrality from one department and transfer it to another. As in the earlier example, if the IS is located in the planning department, the engineering department is likely to lose some of its power by becoming less central to the planning and new product-development activities of the company. Any action or change effort initiated by members of an organization that has the potential to alter the nature of current power relationships provides a tremendous—and perhaps perceived as essential—impetus for political activity.

Why is the study of politics so important for successful IS implementation? The short answer is that the implementation process itself is often highly politicized, as different managers and departments view the development and installation of a new IS as a potentially useful base of power. In other words, any shift in the current operational status quo, such as the introduction of a new system, will inevitably affect how operations and activities are conducted. Once there is a threatened shift in status, departments and managers who perceive themselves as losing power under the new system are apt to do whatever is necessary to discourage or subvert the use of the new system.

Consider a situation in which a city planning department has contracted to install an IS that has the technical ability to perform a wide variety of tasks, including infrastructure tracking and repair, duties originally handled by the city engineering department. However, as a result of the new IS, the city planners now have the capacity to track and schedule road and bridge repair themselves. In this scenario, one would expect the city engineers to do everything they could to either halt the use of the IS, or severely limit it in such a way that it will not interfere with activities they view as their personal responsibility. For example, they might push through a procedural resolution requiring all infrastructure repair planning be done through their office, in spite of the existence of the IS. The essence of the argument is this: With responsibility comes power. If the IS reallocates operational responsibilities, it thereby redefines the power structure.

There are few changes as threatening to organizational members as a redivision of power. Hence, those with a vested interest in the old system will actively resist any efforts to introduce new or innovative changes.

Stakeholder Analysis

Another way to illustrate the essential conflict in IS implementation is through the use of stakeholder analysis, a useful tool for demonstrating some of the seemingly irresolvable conflicts that occur through the planned introduction of any new IS. The concept of an organizational *stakeholder* refers to any individual or group that has an active stake in the success or failure of the planned IS. For example, top management, as a group, once committed to acquiring an IS, has an active stake in ensuring its acceptance and use by client departments. For simplicity, all members of upper management are categorized together as one stakeholder group. A valid argument could be made that there are obviously differing degrees of enthusiasm for and commitment to the adoption of IS technology. In other words, a good deal of conflict and differences of opinion will be discovered within any generalized group. Nevertheless, this approach is useful, because it demonstrates the inherent nature of conflict arising from IS adoption as it exists between stakeholder groups, rather than within any group.

Let us assume that in the case of an effort to implement a new IS there are four identifiable stakeholder groups: 1) top management, 2) the accountant, 3) the clients, and, 4) the manager's own implementation team. Top management has given the initial go-ahead to acquire and install the IS. Likewise, the accountant provides the control and support for the implementation effort, ensuring that budgets are maintained and the project is coming in near projected levels. The clients represent the most obvious stakeholder, as they are the intended recipients of the new system. Finally, assuming an implementation team is working together to implement the IS, it has a stakeholder interest in the implementation, particularly if it is receiving some type of evaluation for its efforts.

To demonstrate the nature of conflict among stakeholder groups, consider three criteria under which the implementation will be evaluated: 1) schedule, 2) budget, and, 3) performance specifications. *Schedule* refers to the projected time frame to complete the installation and get the system online. *Budget* refers to the implementation team's adherence to initial budget figures for the IS adoption. Finally, *performance specifications* involves the assessment that the IS is up and running, performing the range of tasks for which it was acquired. Certainly, additional evaluative criteria can and should be employed; however, for simplicity's sake, these three success measures serve to illustrate the nature of the underlying conflict in any IS implementation.

Figure 6.2 shows the four identified stakeholders and the three success criteria that have been selected. Arrows are used to illustrate the emphasis placed on each of these criteria by the stakeholders. For example, consider stakeholder preferences in terms of the differences between clients and the implementation team. It is obvious that, in terms of evaluation criteria such as schedule and budget, there are significant differences in attitude. The clients want the system delivered as soon as possible for the lowest possible final price. The implementation team would like large budgets and longer installation schedules, because that takes the pressure off the team in terms of bringing the system online. The criterion of performance specifications will vary by stakeholder group. Clients want the opportunity to alter or customize the system, or add as many technical capabilities as is possible. The implementation team is much more comfortable with a simple system that has few technical surprises, is less likely to need long debugging procedures, and is not changed or modified once it has been acquired.

Figure 6.2 presents a compelling case for the underlying conflict of most IS implementation efforts. It also serves to illustrate one inescapable conclusion: In order to rationalize and resolve the varied goals and priorities of the various stakeholders, a considerable amount of bargaining and negotiation is needed. Recall that bargaining and negotiation are two of the primary defining elements of organizational politics. Clearly, political behavior is required in successful implementation efforts. Thinking that a successful project manager will satisfy all stakeholders is expecting too much. Therefore, it is clear that implementation success is predicated on the project manager's ability to successfully bargain and negotiate with the various stakeholders in order to maintain a balance between their needs and the realities of the IS implementation process. Successful implementation becomes a process that depends on the project manager's clever and effective exercise of political skills.

	Cost	Schedule	Performance Specifications
Top Management	↓	↓	—
Accountant	↓	—	—
Client	↓	↓	↑
Implementation Team	↑	↑	↓

Figure 6.2   Stakeholder Analysis

The one important implication of the preceding statement is that project managers tasked with implementing an IS must cultivate the ability to use organizational politics effectively. This does not imply that politics should be practiced in predatory ways; in fact, the approach is likely to seriously backfire on the viability of project managers to develop the trust and goodwill that is needed to implement their systems. Rather, project managers must learn to appreciate and use politics as a negotiating and bargaining tool in pursuit of their ultimate goal: installing the IS. This is another example of how both the politically naive and the shark are equally inappropriate roles for managers to adopt. Successful implementation will not occur without the use of political behavior. Conversely, however, the degree of rancor and bitterness that is usually a byproduct of predatory political behavior is one of the surest ways to torpedo the introduction of a new system.

Managerial Implications—What Do We Do?

An understanding of the political side of organizations and the often intensely political nature of system implementation gives rise to the concomitant need to develop appropriate attitudes and strategies that help project managers operate effectively within the system. If this approach is so necessary to effective IS implementation, what are some steps that project managers can take to become politically astute?

UNDERSTAND AND ACKNOWLEDGE THE POLITICAL NATURE OF MOST ORGANIZATIONS

In dealing with individuals suffering from a variety of dysfunctional problems, therapists and counselors of all types have long taken as their starting point the importance of their patients' acknowledgment that they have a problem. Positive results cannot be achieved in a state of continued denial. Although it is not my purpose to suggest that this analogy holds completely true with organizational politics, the underlying point is still important: Denial of the political nature of organizations does not make that phenomenon any less potent. Organizations in both the public and private sectors are inherently politicized for the reasons that have been previously discussed. This view runs the risk of offending some readers who are uncomfortable with the idea of politics and believe that somehow, through the combined efforts of all organizational actors, it is possible to eradicate the inherently political nature of companies or governmental agencies. The majority of practicing managers (both project and departmental) in organizations today will likely disagree. Politics are too deeply rooted in organizational operations to be treated as some aberrant form of bacteria or diseased tissue that can be excised from the organization's body.

The first implication argues that before managers are able to learn to utilize politics in a manner that is supportive of IS implementation, they must first acknowledge: 1) their existence, and 2) their impact on adoption success. Once we have created a collective basis of understanding regarding the political nature of organizations, it is possible to begin to develop some action steps that will aid in IS implementation.

LEARN TO CULTIVATE APPROPRIATE POLITICAL TACTICS

This principle reinforces the earlier argument that although politics exists, the manner in which organizational actors use politics is the determinant of whether or not the political arena is a healthy or an unhealthy one. There are appropriate and inappropriate methods for using politics. Since the purpose of all political behavior is to develop and keep power, both the politically naive and shark personalities are equally misguided and, perhaps surprisingly, equally damaging to the likelihood of IS implementation success. A project manager who, either through naiveté or stubbornness, refuses to exploit the political arena is destined to be ineffective in introducing the IS. On the other hand, project managers who are so politicized as to appear predatory and aggressive to their colleagues are doomed to create an atmosphere of such distrust and personal animus that there is also little chance for successful IS adoption.

Pursuing the middle ground of political sensibility is the key to system implementation success. An implementation manager who knows how to use politics effectively—that is, to promote the organization's overall goals, which include the development and use of information technologies—is likely to be much more successful in bringing a project to a successful conclusion than either the shark or the naive manager. The process of developing and applying appropriate political tactics means using politics as it can most effectively be used: as a basis for negotiation and bargaining. Politically sensible managers understand that initiating any sort of organizational change, such as that of installing an IS, is bound to reshuffle the distribution of power within the organization. This effect is likely to make many departments and managers very nervous, as they begin to wonder how the future power relationships will be rearranged. Politically sensible implies being sensitive to the concerns (real or imagined) of powerful stakeholder groups; legitimate or not, their concerns about the new IS are real and must be addressed. Appropriate political tactics and behavior include making alliances with powerful members of other stakeholder departments, negotiating mutually acceptable solutions to seemingly insoluble problems, and recognizing that most organizational activities are predicated on the give-and-take of negotiation and compromise. It is through these uses of political behavior that managers of IS implementation efforts put themselves in the position to most effectively influence the successful introduction of their systems.

UNDERSTAND AND ACCEPT *WIIFM*

One of the most difficult lessons for newcomers to organizations to internalize is the consistently expressed and displayed primacy of departmental loyalties and self-interest over organizationwide concerns. Many times novice managers feel frustrated at the *foot-dragging* of other departments and individuals in accepting new ideas or systems that are *good for them*. It is vital that these managers understand that the beauty of a new IS truly is in the eyes of the beholder. One may be absolutely convinced that IS technology will be beneficial to the organization; however, convincing members of other departments of this truth is a different matter altogether.

We must understand that other departments, including system stakeholders, are not likely to offer their help and support of the IS unless they perceive that it is in their best interest to do so. Simply assuming that these departments understand the value of an IS is simplistic and usually wrong. A noted project management consultant, Bob Graham, likes to refer to the principle of *WIIFM*—an acronym for "What's in it for me?"—

when describing the reactions of stakeholder groups to new innovations. This is the question most often asked by individuals and departments when presented with requests for aid and cooperation. They ask why they should help ease the transition period in introducing and using a new system. The worst response for project managers to have is to assume that the stakeholders will automatically appreciate and value the IS as much as they themselves do. Graham's point is that time and care must be taken to use politics effectively, to cultivate a relationship with power holders, and make the deals that need to be made to bring the system online. This is the essence of political sensibility: being level headed enough to have few illusions about the difficulties one is likely to encounter in attempting to install a new IS.

Dealing with System Development Life Cycle Politics

There is a crucial point in time when an organization commits to restarting the system development life cycle (SDLC). Since this decision typically involves allocating significant resources, politics is an obvious issue. The following discussion focuses attention on political forces that can cause premature restarts of the SDLC, and biases in favor of in-house software development.

PREMATURE RESTARTS OF THE SYSTEM DEVELOPMENT LIFE CYCLE

A premature restart of the SDLC simply means that an existing system gets scrapped too early. Although replacing an old system with a new one can provide opportunities to fix problems, add functionality, and leverage better and cheaper technology, it is wrong to push this proposition to its extreme. Throwing away an existing system means throwing away a significant capital investment; it is also a disruptive, costly, and risky undertaking. Furthermore, if an organization can stretch the use of an existing system, the eventual restart will benefit from cheaper and better technology.

Given that each system has an ideal point in time when the benefits of the replacement outweigh the costs, it is important to understand the organizational dynamics that might lead to deviations from that point. Let us start by asking who stands to gain from a premature scrapping of an existing system.

Replacing existing systems can obviously benefit IS managers and their staffs. The restart of the SDLC provides IS management with a bonanza of bigger budgets and bigger staffs. Besides the obvious resources required for the development process, we cannot ignore the need to support the existing system, can we?

Being in charge of a larger and richer IS department is only part of the fun. IS people thrive on the excitement and challenges of learning and applying new technologies to the development of new systems. What sounds better to you: "Maintain a COBOL purchasing system" or "Develop a three-tier, thin-client, object-oriented, rule-based, E-commerce requisitioning system"? Besides being exciting, the development of such new systems is also rewarding from the point of view of pay, job security, and résumé building.

So, can we assume that management in other organizational areas would act as a counterbalance to these biases? Unfortunately, the answer is no. Managers in all areas of the organization are exposed to an ongoing stream of complaints and maintenance costs associated with the deficiencies of the existing system (see the Management Information System Zoo discussion in Chapter 3). In the absence of signals indicating the long-term viability of the existing system, it is easy for managers to be biased toward scrapping the existing system. In addition, the development of a new system may offer managers and staff in the affected functional areas opportunities to participate in a process that can contribute to their careers and job satisfaction, and to claim a greater portion of the organizational resources. This is particularly true when the development cost is not charged to their respective organizational units but is borne by the organization as a whole.

Note that we are not ignoring the famous *resistance-to-change* factor that would work against the pursuit of a new system. However, our experience shows that the people who resist change are typically at lower levels of the organization, and hence their influence is felt more at the development stage, as opposed to the decision phase.

Finally, we would like to mention one more potential source of bias toward premature scrapping of existing systems—the arrival of a new executive. We have witnessed cases when a new executive pushed for the replacement of an existing system for political reasons. In some cases, the executive wanted to remove traces of the previous *alpha-manager*—who was the champion of the existing system. In other cases, the executive wanted to respond decisively to complaints about the existing system, or simply wanted to make a mark as a strong leader who can affect significant change.

Biases Favoring In-House Software Development

Information systems managers and staff may favor in-house software development over purchasing software packages for the same obvious reasons that they favor software development over software maintenance.

While managers of other organizational units and top executives may have no such vested interests in the matter, they are not well equipped to argue the matter. If the IS people say our business processes are unique and that integrating the available packages with our existing systems would be too costly, who is to argue against that?

WHAT CAN YOU DO ABOUT THESE BIASES?

Since internal politics are biased toward premature restarts of the SDLC and in-house software development, external forces are required to keep things in balance. The CEO or the IS steering committee should insist on a review by external consultants before approving any significant software expenditure.

We are aware of one case when this procedure saved a government millions of dollars. In 1974, the IS group in charge of running the government payroll system convinced everyone involved that the system was about to collapse and was no longer maintainable. Since the expenditure for redeveloping the system was very large, top government officials contracted with an external IS consultant to review the situation and submit a report in support of the proposed project.

To everyone's surprise, the consultant submitted a report stating that if a number of reasonable steps were taken, the life of the system could be extended by ten years. The IS group suggested that the consultant be admitted for observations at the closest psychiatric clinic; yet, the consultant's recommendations were accepted and put into action.

Twenty years later, in 1994, the same payroll system was still being used, though most of the modules had been gradually rewritten. At that point, and after getting the blessing from the same external consultant, a request for proposals for the replacement of the system was issued. The total savings from extending the life of the system are estimated at more than ten million dollars.

Conclusions

Implementation politics is a process that few managers, even adept ones, enjoy. Interviews and conversations with a variety of managers across a diverse collection of public and private organizations have made it clear that using politics, even in the *sensible* manner suggested in this chapter, is a distasteful process for most managers.

Most of us do not enjoy having to cut deals, negotiate the introduction of new systems, and constantly mollify departmental heads who are suspicious of the motives behind installing an IS—or any other system that threatens their power base. Nevertheless, the realities of modern organizations are such that successful managers must learn to use the political process for their own purposes; it is simply wishful thinking to assume otherwise.

This chapter lays out some of the major issues in organizational politics. It defines and identifies some of its reasons for existence, as well as suggesting some guidelines for effectively managing IS implementation within the political context of organizations. Its goal has been to offer some practical views on the nature and importance of political behavior in modern organizations. If one additional reader becomes better attuned to the political realties of corporate life as a result of what she has read, this chapter has accomplished its goal.

7

Team Building and Cross-Functional Cooperation: Setting the Stage for Success

> Cooperation is everything: freckles would make a nice tan coat if they'd get together.
>
> *Anonymous*

One difficulty confronting most project managers has so far been mentioned only in passing: developing and maintaining the productivity of the team of individuals installing the new system. The difficulties involved in building and coordinating an effective team are daunting, and inattention to these demands has caused many implementation efforts to fail. What often makes this set of duties so frustrating for many project managers is that they have received extensive training in the technical aspects of their jobs, but often have little knowledge of the *human* side of their responsibilities. Specifically, the efforts involved in building and maintaining cooperation among disparate individuals have been and remain a considerable challenge. Many managers, uncomfortable with these duties, often are willing to turn a blind eye to their execution, perhaps under the mistaken belief that the rest of the team members are professionals willing to put the implementation effort first, and bury past conflicts and animosities.

Unfortunately—as discussed previously, on organizational politics—the reverse is often the case. While nominally being a member of the team, usually composed of members from different functional departments or with varying degrees of technical training, individuals still retain loyalties to the concerns and interests of their own functional departments. Consequently, in addition to harboring prejudices about members of other functional groups, team members often view their primary responsibility as being to their own functional group rather than to the implementation team. This then is the challenge that is faced by information system (IS) managers: how to take a disparate group of individuals with different backgrounds, attitudes, and goals and mold them into a *team* in every sense of the word.

It is important to note at the outset that this chapter is intended to offer some prescriptive advice to project managers on the topic of team building. It goes without saying that project managers who function as sole supporters and implementers of their companies' or agencies' IS should use this material to create a cohesive relationship with the client, for they are in fact the project team. Certainly, team building is most useful when managers have a team that they need to manage as effectively as possible. However, for some IS managers, the team will be composed of themselves and a client group, rather than a set of subordinates. Consequently, this topic is for all those readers who are about to make use of teams as part of their implementation effort.

Characteristics of Effective Teams

A great deal of research has investigated the qualities that effective teams possess and the degree to which those same qualities are missing from less effective groups. While much has been written, there are a great many aspects of successful teams that these sources share in common. Briefly, the most common underlying features of successful implementation teams tend to be: 1) a clear sense of mission, 2) an understanding of interdependencies, 3) cohesiveness, 4) trust among team members, and, 5) a shared sense of enthusiasm.

A Clear Sense of Mission

As Chapter 4, on critical success factors, demonstrated, one of the key determinants of implementation success is a clear project mission. Further, that sense of mission must be mutually understood and accepted by all team members. In fact, research on J. K. Pinto and Slevin's ten-critical-success-factor model not only demonstrates the existence of this factor, but it also shows that it was the number-one predictor of project implementation success among the ten critical factors. Team members need a purpose around which to rally. They must have some sense of the overall goals that drive the IS implementation. Experience with system implementation successes and failures has very clearly differentiated the efficacy of team performance in both the presence and absence of overall goals. Likewise, it is key that not only should the implementation team leader know the goals, but also that this knowledge must be shared by all concerned parties.

A common but often tragic mistake made by many managers—particularly those who are insecure about their authority vis-à-vis the project team—is to segment the team members in terms of their duties, giving each a small, well-specified task but with no sense of how that activity contributes to the overall IS implementation effort. This approach is a serious mistake for several important reasons.

First, the implementation team is the manager's best source of troubleshooting for problems, both potential and actual. If the team is kept in the dark, members who could potentially help with the smooth transition of the IS through participating in other aspects of the installation are not able to contribute in helpful ways.

Second, team members know and resent when they are being kept in the dark about various features of the system's implementation. Consciously or not, when project managers keep their teams isolated and involved in fragmented tasks, they are sending a signal that they either do not trust the team, or do not feel that the team has the competence to address issues related to the overall implementation effort. Finally, from a *fire-fighting* perspective, it simply makes good sense for team leaders to keep their people abreast of the status of the project. The more time spent defining goals and clarifying roles in the initial stages of the team's development, the less time that will be needed to resolve problems and adjudicate disputes down the road.

UNDERSTANDING THE TEAM'S INTERDEPENDENCIES

This characteristic refers to the degree of knowledge that team members have and the importance that they attach to the interrelatedness of their efforts. Interdependence refers to the degree of joint activity among team members that is required in order to bring the IS online. In many situations, a team leader may be required to form a team with members from various functional areas within the organization. For example, a typical IS introduction at a large corporation could conceivably require the development of a team that included members from management information systems, engineering, accounting, marketing, and administration. As the concept of differentiation suggests, each of these individuals brings to the team preconceived notions of the roles that each should play, the importance of the various contributions, and other parochial attitudes. Acquiring an understanding of mutual interdependencies implies developing a mutual level of appreciation for the strengths and contributions that each team member brings to the table, and is a necessary precondition for team success. Team members must become aware not only of their own contributions, but also of how their work fits into the overall scheme of the IS installation and, further, how it relates to the other necessary work of team members from other departments.

COHESIVENESS

Cohesiveness, at its most basic, simply refers to the degree of mutual attraction that team members hold for each other and their tasks. In other words, it is the strength of desire that all members have to remain a team. In the chapter on political behavior, we discussed the concept of WIIFM, that is, the basic question often asked by organizational members prior to volunteering their services: What's in it for me? In many ways, cohesiveness is built and strengthened by appealing to WIIFM in team members. It is safe to assume that most members of the implementation team need a reason or reasons to contribute their skills and time to the successful adoption of the IS. When asked to serve on the implementation team and actively contribute to the process, they search for what's in it for them to do so. It is important not to feel betrayed by any initial lack of enthusiasm on their parts, as it is understandable and predictable. Part of the job of an implementation team leader is to instill in the team a sense of and answers to WIIFM. It directly affects his efforts toward establishing a degree of cohesiveness and solidarity as a project team. Project managers work to build a team that is cohesive as a starting point for performing their tasks. Since cohesiveness is predicated on the attraction that the group holds for each individual member, managers need to make use of all resources at their disposal, including reward systems, recognition, performance appraisals, and any other sources of organizational reward to induce team members to devote time and energy to furthering the team's goals.

TRUST

Trust means different things to different people. For a project team, trust can best be understood as the team's comfort level with each individual member. Given that comfort level, trust is manifested in the team's ability and willingness to squarely address differences of opinion, values, and attitudes and to deal with them accordingly. Trust is the common denominator without which ideas of group cohesion and appreciation become moot.

Consider the situation of any implementation effort involving personnel from a variety of departments. Conflict and disagreements among team members are not only likely but also should be treated as a given. Trust is embodied in the belief of various team members that they are able to raise issues of conflict and disagreement without concern for retaliation or other sanctions. Because intragroup conflicts are so frequent within project teams, the manner with which they are dealt is often a determinant of the group's ultimate success or failure. Managers make a big mistake in trying to submerge or put off disagreements and conflict, believing that they are counterproductive to group activities. In a sense, these managers are correct: No one wants conflicts among members of a team. On the other hand, they are missing the larger picture that reveals the inevitability of these conflicts. The mark of managerial success lies not in dampening conflict, but in causing conflict to surface and the manner in which that conflict, once having arisen, is handled. It is through establishing trust among team members that conflicts and other disagreements over procedures or activities can be most effectively discussed and concluded with a minimal loss of time and energy.

ENTHUSIASM

Enthusiasm is the key to creating the energy and spirit that drives effective implementation efforts. The point that the project team leader needs to keep emphasizing among team members is that they can achieve the goals set for them. This point is best illustrated by a recently witnessed example. A team leader had been charged with installing a geographic information system in the planning and development office of a large city government. Despite his initial enthusiasm and energy, he was getting increasingly frustrated with his project team members, most who had been assigned to him without any of his input. His chief concern became how to deal with the constant litany of "We can't do that here," which he heard every time he offered a suggestion for changing a procedure or trying anything new. One Monday morning, his team members walked into the office to the vision of the words, "Yes We Can!", painted in letters three feet high across one wall of the office. (Over the weekend, the team leader had come in and done a little redecorating.) From that point on, the motto, Yes We Can!, became the theme of the implementation team and had a wonderful impact on adoption success.

This story illustrates an important point: Enthusiasm starts at the top. If the team senses that the leader is only going through the motions or has little optimism for system success, his sense of apathy is quickly communicated to the team and soon pervades all its activities. The team cannot be fooled; it senses when managers truly believe in the IS and when they do not.

Stages in Group Development

The importance of molding an effective implementation team is further supported by research that argues that the group development process is a dynamic one (Tuchman and Jensen 1977). Groups go through several maturation stages that are often readily identifiable, are generally found across a variety of organizations, and involve groups formed for a variety of different purposes. (These stages are illustrated in Table 7.1.)

STAGE ONE: FORMING

The first step in group development consists of collecting individuals to form the group. Forming consists of the process or approaches used in order to mold a collection of individuals into a coherent team. Team members begin to get acquainted with each other, talk about the purposes of the group, how and what types of leadership patterns will be used, and what will be acceptable behaviors within the group. In essence, forming constitutes the *rule-setting* stage, when the ground rules for interaction (who is really in charge and how members are expected to interact) and activity (how productive members are expected to be) are established and mutually agreed upon. It is important that this step be completed early in the group's life in order to eliminate ambiguities further along in the implementation process. In many instances, the role of the team leader will be to create structure for these early meetings, as well as to set the tone for future cooperation and positive member attitudes.

STAGE TWO: STORMING

Storming refers to the natural reaction to these initial ground rules, as members begin to test the limits and constraints placed on their behavior. Storming is a conflict-laden stage in which the preliminary leadership patterns, reporting relationships, and norms of work and interpersonal behavior are challenged and, perhaps, reestablished. During this stage, it is likely that the team leader will begin to see a number of the group members demonstrating personal agendas (don't forget WIIFM) and prejudices. These behaviors are bound to create a level of hostility and conflict among team members, which the leader must be prepared to address.

It is also important to note that the process of storming is a very natural phase through which all groups go. One of the worst things that the leader can do when confronted with storming behavior is to attempt to suppress that behavior through ridicule—"Why don't you both start acting like adults?"—or appeals to professionalism—"We are all on the same side"—in the hope that members will be shamed or coaxed into dropping the conflict. This approach almost never works, because it simply pushes the

Stage	Defining Characteristics
1. Forming	Members get to know each other and lay the basis for project ground rules.
2. Storming	Conflicts begin as members come to resist authority, demonstrate hidden agendas and prejudices.
3. Norming	Members agree on operating procedures, seeking to work together, developing close relationships, and committing to the implementation process.
4. Performing	Group members work together to accomplish their tasks.
5. Adjourning	Groups may disband either following the installation or through group member reassignments.

Table 7.1   Stages in Group Development

conflict below the surface. Consequently, team members who have not been allowed to resolve difficulties during an active storming phase may begin engaging in a campaign of guerrilla warfare against each other, constantly sniping or denigrating each other's contributions to the implementation effort. Taken to its extreme, unresolved conflict can sink the implementation process, as it reduces the group's efforts to ineffectiveness.

Project team leaders should acknowledge storming behavior for what it is, and treat it as a serious but ultimately healthy sign of team growth and maturation. One of the most productive behaviors in which leaders can engage is to provide a forum for group members to air concerns and complaints without indulging in judgmental behavior. The team leader acting as a problem solver and coach is likely to be far more effective in building a productive team than the manager who views all intragroup conflict with alarm, and actively seeks to suppress it in the mistaken hope that, if ignored, it will simply go away.

STAGE 3: NORMING

A *norm* is most often defined as an unwritten rule of behavior. Norming behavior in a group implies that the team members are establishing mutually agreed-to practices and attitudes. Norms serve to help the team determine how it should make decisions, how often it should meet, the degree of openness and trust that team members will exhibit toward each other, and how conflicts will be resolved. Research has shown that it is during the norming stage that the cohesiveness of the group grows to its highest level. Close relationships develop, a sense of mutual concern and appreciation emerges, and feelings of camaraderie and shared responsibility become evident. The norming stage establishes the playing field upon which the actual work of the team will commence.

STAGE 4: PERFORMING

It is during the performing stage that the actual *work* of the implementation team is performed or executed. It is only when the first three phases have been properly accomplished that the team will have reached the level of maturity and confidence to effectively perform its duties.

One of the most common mistakes made by novice project managers is pushing the team immediately into the work of the implementation plan. Typically, this approach consists of holding an initial meeting to get acquainted, parceling out the work, and essentially telling the team members to get started with their pieces of the process. The reason this approach, although quite erroneous, is so often used can be attributed to the impatience of top management and the team leader who wants to be *doing something*. The real fear that these IS implementation leaders exhibit is linked to the expectation of top management's retribution, based on the belief that top management expects results. Naturally, this assumption is correct, to a degree. However, bear in mind that what top management is expecting is a successfully implemented IS. Its rightful concern is with the results, not the process. A more seasoned manager, while taking the time to develop a productive implementation team, is also communicating with top management to keep it informed on the progress of team development, as part of the IS installation. It is only when top management knows nothing of what a manager is doing that it assumes that the manager is doing nothing (Graham 1992).

STAGE 5: ADJOURNING

Adjourning recognizes the fact that implementation does not last forever. At some point, the IS has been installed, the team is disbanded, and members return to their functional duties within the organization. In some cases, the group may downsize slowly and deliberately. For example, as various components of the IS come online, a team that contains a cost accountant may no longer require that individual's services, and she will be reassigned. In other circumstances, the team will complete its tasks and be disbanded completely. In either case, it is important to remember that during the final stages of the implementation process group members are likely to be exhibiting some concern about their future assignments and/or new duties. Project managers need to be sensitive to the valid concerns felt by these team members and, when possible, help to smooth the transition from the old team to new assignments.

WHAT STAGE ARE YOU IN?

In addition to presenting the group-development stages, the previously mentioned information also attempts to describe some of the leadership duties that are a necessary part of project managers' jobs. The moral of this message for project managers is to pay particular attention to the stage that the implementation team is currently addressing, and tailor leadership behaviors to facilitate the successful completion of that stage. For example, during the early stages of forming and storming, project managers can be most effective when they play the dual roles of developing task assignments and nurturing and influencing interpersonal relationships. In other words, they need to foster a combination of work and people skills, as they set the agenda for the implementation effort within the context of the human interactions that are bound to lead to conflict and disagreement. On the other hand, later in the team's implementation efforts, the leader can begin to develop a more exclusive goal-oriented style. Assuming that the leader has spent adequate time developing the team, by the performing stage, the leader can devote time almost entirely to creating a work-related atmosphere. Finally, in the adjourning stage of the project, leaders should again become aware of and use their people skills as the implementation project starts to *ramp down* toward completion. It goes without saying that this combination of people and task skills is difficult to develop. Further, it is even more arduous, particularly for new IS managers, to know when to differentially employ them. Nevertheless, the mark of successful team leaders is often: 1) their acknowledgment that the team development process is dynamic, and, 2) their leadership style can and must change at appropriate points to address the relevant issues that have surfaced. These issues will be discussed in detail in Chapter 8.

Achieving Cross-Functional Cooperation

Many IS implementation teams are staffed by a skilled but disparate group of organizational members. Because these members come from a variety of different backgrounds and are inculcated with certain beliefs and value sets of their functional departments, the challenge of creating a viable, cohesive team out of these different individuals is often daunting. We have examined the characteristics of effective teams, as well as how team attitudes and behaviors change across various, identifiable stages in group maturation. However, we have not yet examined exactly how one begins to create cohesion, trust, enthusiasm, and other characteristics of winning teams. In other words, what are some tactics that managers can employ to encourage the type of effective team development that will aid in IS implementation?

The following discusses factors that were identified as part of a recent research project investigating the causes of cross-functional cooperation on project teams (M. B. Pinto 1988). The study affirmed the importance of a set of factors that can help encourage cross-functional cooperation and, further, offered some managerial implications that will be discussed below.

SUPERORDINATE GOALS

Every organization and manager has more than one goal that guides activities and actions. Often, project managers are faced with trying to resolve situations in which team members from different functional areas perceive conflicting goals for an implementation effort. For example, consider the implementation of IS technology in a local government. For this project, accounting's primary goal is to minimize cost while engineering's primary goal is to enlarge the range of applications in hopes of increasing client satisfaction and, therefore, use of the system. In order for this implementation effort to be successful, one functional area may be required to sacrifice, or at least compromise, its primary goals. Aware of these areas of potential cross-functional conflict, managers charged with the responsibility for implementation success are continually looking for ways to develop goals that increase, rather than detract from, cross-functional cooperation.

A *superordinate goal* refers to an overall goal or purpose that is important to all functional groups involved, but its attainment requires the resources and efforts of more than one group (Sherif 1958). The superordinate goal is an addition to, not a replacement for, other goals that the functional groups may have set. The premise is that when project team members from different functional areas share an overall goal or common purpose, they tend to cooperate toward this end. To illustrate, let us return to the example of IS implementation in a local business. A superordinate goal for this project team may be "to develop a high quality, user-friendly, and generally useful IS that will enhance the operations of various departments and functions." This overall goal attempts to enhance, or pull together, some of the diverse function-specific goals for cost effectiveness, schedule adherence, quality, and innovation. It provides a central objective or an overriding goal toward which the entire project team can strive.

RULES AND PROCEDURES

Rules and procedures are central to any discussion of cross-functional cooperation because they offer a means for coordinating or integrating activities that involve several functional units (Galbraith 1977). For years, organizations have relied on rules and procedures to link the activities of organizational members. Rules and procedures have been used to assign duties, evaluate performance, resolve conflicts, and so on. Rules and procedures can be used to address formalized rules and procedures established by the organization for the performance of the implementation process, as well as project-specific rules and procedures developed by the project team to facilitate its operations.

In some instances, project teams do not have the luxury of relying on established rules and procedures to assist members with their tasks. Therefore, they often create their own rules and procedures to facilitate the progress of the project. Organizational rules and procedures are defined as formalized rules and procedures established by the organization that mandate or control the activities of the project team in terms of team membership, task assignment, and performance evaluation. Project team rules and procedures, on the other hand, refer to the degree to which the project team must establish its own rules and procedures to facilitate the progress of the project. For example, one such rule could be that all project team members will make themselves available to each other regarding project business. It is likely that greater levels of cross-functional cooperation will result from the establishment of these rules and procedures.

PHYSICAL PROXIMITY

Both the literature and common observations seem to suggest that individuals are more likely to interact and communicate with others when the physical characteristics of buildings or settings encourage them to do so (Davis 1984). For example, the sheer size and spatial layout of a building can affect working relationships. In a small building, or when a work group is clustered on the same floor, relationships tend to be more intimate since people are in close physical proximity to each other. As people spread along corridors or among different buildings, interactions may become less frequent and/or less spontaneous. In these situations, it is more difficult for employees to interact with members of their own department or other departments.

Many companies seriously consider the potential effects of physical proximity on project-team cooperation. In fact, some project organizations relocate personnel working together on a project to the same office or floor. These organizations contend that when individuals work near each other, they are more likely to communicate and, ultimately, cooperate with each other.

ACCESSIBILITY

While physical proximity is important to the study of cross-functional cooperation, another factor, accessibility, appears to be an equally important predictor of the phenomenon. Accessibility is the perception by others that a person is approachable for communication and interaction on problems or concerns that are related to the success of a project. Separate from the issue of physical proximity, accessibility refers to additional factors that can inhibit the amount of interaction that occurs between organizational members—e.g., an individual's schedule, position in an organization, or out-of-office commitments (Peters 1986). These factors often affect accessibility among organizational members.

For example, consider a public-sector organization in which a member of the engineering department is physically located near a member of the city's census department. While these individuals are in close proximity to one another, they may rarely interact because of different work schedules, varied duties and priorities, and commitment to their own agendas. These factors often create a perception of inaccessibility among the individuals involved.

Implications for Project Managers

The results of the previously mentioned research study suggest some pragmatic implications for project managers who are interested in increasing cooperation among project team members.

COOPERATION IS A VITAL ELEMENT IN IMPLEMENTATION SUCCESS

Cross-functional cooperation can truly result in higher levels of project implementation performance. In other words, to follow the model presented in Figure 7.1, there is a strong link between cross-functional cooperation and successful IS implementation outcomes. While this result should not be surprising to most project managers, the strength of the relationship between cooperation and implementation success has important implications. For example, because cooperation is so important for project success, factors that facilitate cross-functional cooperation will also greatly enhance the likelihood of successful IS installation and adoption. In other words, cooperation is more than an element in project success; it is often the key link in helping managers develop a project team that is both capable and motivated to successfully develop and implement the IS.

SUPERORDINATE GOALS REPRESENT A STRONG PREDICTOR OF CROSS-FUNCTIONAL COOPERATION

Superordinate goals are clearly important in attaining cross-functional cooperation among project team members. In fact, superordinate goals comprise the strongest individual predictor of cooperation. Project managers must reinforce overriding goals—goals toward which the entire implementation team as a whole must work.

Superordinate goals require the combined efforts of different members of the project team. One individual or subgroup independently attaining the goals is not helpful to fostering cooperation.

These goals need to be clearly defined. Vague goals can result in increased confusion rather than clarity. For example, an insurance company recently promoted an overall goal among its functional departments to become "number one in our industry." The marketing department interpreted the goal to mean increasing sales volume as high as possible, regardless of gross margins and profitability. The accounting and actuarial department, on the other hand, interpreted this goal to mean squeezing as much profit as possible by raising rates on policies to the point when it was losing market share through declining sales. In this example, the vagueness in defining a superordinate goal actually worked against the organization.

There are many examples of projects in which superordinate goals may have existed, but were never adequately communicated to the important project team members. In these cases, the goals were conveyed only to a small, select group rather than to all impacted individuals. For example, in a recent *Fortune* interview, the former chief executive officer and chairman of General Motors, Roger Smith, discussed his decision to spend billions of dollars revitalizing manufacturing facilities. When asked if he would have done anything differently, he replied:

> I sure wish I'd done a better job of communicating with GM people.
> I'd ... make sure they understood and shared my vision for the

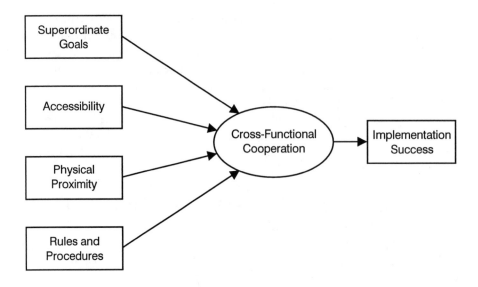

Figure 7.1   Antecedents and Consequences of Cross-Functional Cooperation

company. ... If people understand the why, they'll work at it. I never got all this across. There we were, charging up the hill right on schedule, and I looked behind me and saw that many people were still at the bottom, trying to decide whether to come along. (*Fortune* 1989, 71)

It is important to note that superordinate goals are not intended as a substitute for other project goals. By definition, superordinate goals are overriding and are intended to complement, rather than replace, other specific project-team goals. Consequently, project team members from different functional areas may still hold to some of their own specific departmental goals while also being committed to the overall project or common goal of the project.

SET POLICIES TO ENSURE THAT TEAM MEMBERS REMAIN ACCESSIBLE TO EACH OTHER

An important way to promote cooperation among members of the project team is to ensure that they remain accessible to each other, both during and outside of their project duties. A variety of methods can be used to encourage such accessibility including establishing regular project meetings, setting formal channels of communication, and encouraging informal get-togethers, e.g., in the hall, over coffee, and at lunch. It is important that team leaders promote an atmosphere in which team members feel that they can approach or meet with other team members outside of the formally developed hierarchical channels or project meeting times. One suggestion for promoting an atmosphere of accessibility surfaced during an interview with a project manager, who commented on the need to create a "priority status" for the project: "I try to convey a sense of urgency about this project to my team members. I want them to give this project 'priority status.' When something is a priority, then they will find the time necessary to devote to it" (Pregent 1988).

PHYSICAL PROXIMITY IS AN IMPORTANT SUPPLEMENTAL FACTOR FOR ACHIEVING COOPERATION

In addition to fostering an atmosphere of accessibility, project managers may wish to relocate team members to improve accessibility and cooperation. The importance of physical proximity for cooperation stems from the contention that when individuals work near each other, they are more likely to interact, communicate, and cooperate with each other. A member of Corning Glass' engineering office noted, "Engineers get more than 80 percent of their ideas through direct, face-to-face contact with their peers. They will not travel more than 100 feet from their desks to exchange ideas ... and they hate to use the telephone to seek information" (Leibson 1981, 8).

WORK TO ESTABLISH STANDARD OPERATING RULES AND PROCEDURES FOR THE PROJECT TEAM

Rules and procedures determine exactly how members of different departments and functional areas interact with other project team members. If managers set standardized rules of behavior, they can better control and facilitate the degree and quality of cross-functional cooperation. One project manager established a policy that "all major changes to the information system, either scheduling, budgetary, or technical, will require input from and active involvement of project team representatives from each functional department." When followed consistently, this type of operating procedure is a very simple yet effective method for promoting cross-functional cooperation.

Because of the relative simplicity of the use of rules and procedures as a tool for encouraging cross-functional cooperation, some organizations tend to over-rely on this method while ignoring other techniques that have been discussed, such as project member accessibility, physical proximity, or the creation of superordinate goals. While it is true that each of these factors has been found to lead to enhanced cross-functional cooperation, project managers should not simply choose the technique or factor that is most available or easiest to implement. To truly create and maintain an atmosphere in which cross-functional cooperation can thrive within the project team, it is highly advisable to make use of a combination of all of the factors, including superordinate goals, accessibility, and rules and procedures. Used individually, they may be helpful to the project manager. Used in conjunction with each other, they represent a significantly more powerful tool for creating a cooperative business climate and, consequently, aiding in project success.

Conclusions

This chapter discusses some of the important issues in developing and maintaining effective implementation teams. Team building and development are important and ongoing challenges for project managers because, while often time consuming, it can reap large dividends. A basis for understanding the factors that characterize successful teams is presented. The various stages of team development are argued to be not only an important but also a healthy sign of implementation team performance. Finally, some practical advice on promoting cross-functional cooperation among team members is provided.

Experience, research, and anecdotal evidence confirm that IS implementation is difficult and complex. Many issues and factors go into creating a project team atmosphere conducive to successful IS implementation. Team development and cooperation among project team members is essential, particularly when the project team is composed of members from various functional departments. These practical approaches to fostering better cross-functional cooperation can lead to more effective IS implementation efforts.

8

Leadership and Project Success

There are few topics as widely discussed and engender such controversy and disagreement as leadership behavior. Book after book has been written attempting to show how all managers can become better leaders, how leadership is the key to organizational and even national renewal, and how leadership, particularly when exercised throughout the organization in the form of empowerment, can lead to enhanced competitiveness and quality. Trying to help project managers become better leaders will always be a difficult task.

Project managers charged with implementing systems must rely on a variety of skills. Because the implementation process is intensely people oriented, some of the most important skills to be developed are the abilities to motivate, inspire, and lead the team.

Time and again, true project manager leadership has been shown to be one of the most important characteristics in successful implementation not just because its impact is felt within the team, but also because it has an impact on other managers and important information systems (IS) stakeholders (Slevin and J. K. Pinto 1988; Posner 1987; J. K. Pinto et al. 1998). As a result, the more we are able to understand about the dynamics of this concept, the better we will be able to effectively manage our implementation projects and train a future generation of managers in the required tasks and skills.

Leadership is a complex process that is crucial to successful system implementation. The principal difficulty with studying leadership is that we know at once so much and so little about the concept. Behavioral scientists have been studying the leadership problem over the past half-century in an attempt to better understand the processes and to come up with some prescriptive recommendations concerning effective leadership behaviors. Years of careful research have generated a variety of findings that at best is sometimes confusing to the practicing manager and, at worst, is often internally inconsistent. For example, the following eleven propositions have all been suggested to guide leadership behavior.

1. Leaders will be most effective when they show a high level of concern for both the task and the employees, their subordinates (Blake and Mouton 1964).

2. Leaders should be task oriented when they have either high or low control over the group. When they have only moderate control over the group, leaders should be people oriented (Fiedler 1978).

3. To be effective, leaders must base their decision-making style on how important employee acceptance of the decision will be. Accordingly, they should seek participation by subordinates in decision-making (Vroom and Yetton 1973).

4. Leaders will be accepted and will motivate employees to the extent that their behavior helps employees progress toward valued goals and provides guidance or clarification not already present in the work situation (House 1971).

5. A participative approach to leadership will lead to improved employee morale and increase their commitment to the organization (Fleishman 1973).

6. Under stressful conditions (e.g., time pressure), an autocratic leadership style will lead to greater productivity (Fodor 1976). A minimum level of friendliness or warmth will enhance this effect (Tjosvold 1984).

7. Even when the leader has all the needed information to make a decision and the problem is clearly structured, employees prefer a participative approach to decision-making (Heilman et al. 1984).

8. Effective leaders tend to exhibit high levels of intelligence, initiative, personal needs for occupational achievement, and self confidence (Stogdill 1984).

9. Effective leadership behavior can depend on the organizational setting. Thus, similar behaviors may have different consequences in different settings (Ghiselli 1971).

10. Leadership behavior may not be important if subordinates are skilled, if tasks are structured or routine, if technology dictates the required actions, or if the administrative climate is supportive and fair (Dansereau et al. 1975).

11. Leadership behavior can be divided into task behavior (one-way communication) and relationship behavior (two-way communication). An effective leadership style using these behaviors can be selected,

according to the maturity level of subordinates relative to accomplishing the task (Salancik et al. 1975).

This list of principles of leadership and leader behavior presents a bewildering set of premises for managers. In some cases, these points seem to actively disagree with each other. For example, some researchers say that a participatory leadership style is best for all situations, while other works suggest that a participatory style is more effective in some situations and with some types of subordinates than in others. Some researchers argue that specific leader character traits determine effectiveness, while others state that it is in fact the dynamics of the leader's interaction with subordinates that determines effectiveness. Finally, other authors have concluded that, under some conditions, leadership style is not important at all (Kerr and Jermier 1978).

So where does this leave the project manager? These research results certainly reinforce the perception that the process of leadership is confusing, complex, and often contradictory. What would help the project manager is a day-to-day working model that clarifies some aspects of the concept of leadership, suggests alternative leadership styles that may be used, and provides some practical recommendations for conditions under which alternative leadership styles might be used. This chapter describes an approach to leadership that will help the implementation team leader consciously select the leadership style appropriate for alternative situations.

Leadership Behavior and Project Management: What We Know

Besides the collection of prescriptive studies listed earlier, which argue for specific leader-related actions, we can investigate the results of large-scale leadership research aimed at uncovering those traits specific to leaders. Because a leader is not the same thing as a manager per se, we find *leaders* in all walks of life and occupying all levels within organizational hierarchies. A recent study, which sought to uncover traits that most managers feel are important for leaders to possess, is particularly illuminating. A large sample survey was used to ask a total of 2,615 managers within United States (U.S.) corporations what they considered to be the most important characteristics of effective leaders (Kouzes and Posner 1991).

Table 8.1 presents the results of this survey. A significant majority of managers felt that the most important characteristic of superior leaders is basic honesty. They seek leaders who say what they mean and live up to their promises. In addition, they seek competence and intelligence, vision, inspiration, fairness, imagination, and dependability, to names a few of the most important characteristics listed. These traits offer an

Characteristic	Ranking	Percentage of Managers Selecting
Honest	1	83
Competent	2	67
Forward-Looking	3	62
Inspiring	4	58
Intelligent	5	43
Fair-Minded	6	40
Broad-Minded	7	37
Straightforward	8	34
Imaginative	9	34
Dependable	10	33

From Kouzes and Posner (1991)

Table 8.1   Characteristics of Effective Leaders

important starting point toward a better understanding of how leaders operate and, more importantly, how the other members of the project team or organization expect them to operate. Clearly, the most important factors we seek in leaders are the dimensions of trust, strength of character, and the intelligence and competence to succeed. The expectation of success is important; the majority of followers do not tag along after failures for very long.

Another study on leadership roles of senior executives has revealed five broad categories of leadership roles, as perceived by their subordinates (Javidan and Dastmachian 1993). These roles include 1) ambassador, 2) visionary, 3) driver, 4) mobilizer, and, 5) servant. The results of the large-scale study (1,687 senior to upper-middle managers in three large Canadian firms were polled) led to the following conclusion: The hierarchical level of the superior and the nature of the organization itself both influence the effective mix of leadership roles. That is, within some firms and at certain management levels, effective leaders use certain roles (e.g., driver versus servant) to a greater degree.

There is research specifically related to project managers and the leadership traits necessary to be successful in this more specialized arena. Two studies in particular shed some valuable light on the nature of the special demands facing project managers and the concomitant nature of the leadership characteristics they must manifest. One analyzed data from a number of sources and synthesized a set of factors that most effective project leaders shared in common (Pettersen 1991). It identified five important characteristics for proficient project management: 1) oral communication skills, 2) influencing skills, 3) intellectual capabilities, 4) the ability to handle stress, and, 5) diverse management skills, including planning, delegation, and decision-making. Most project managers do not have the capacity to exercise power that derives from formal positional authority; consequently, they are forced to develop effective influencing skills.

The second study also identified five characteristics closely associated with effective project team leaders (Einsiedel 1987):

1. Credibility: Is the project manager trustworthy and taken seriously by both the project team and the parent organization?

2. Creative problem solver: Is the project manager skilled at problem analysis and identification?

3. Tolerance for ambiguity: Is the project manager adversely affected by complex or ambiguous (uncertain) situations?

4. Flexible management style: Is the project manager able to handle rapidly changing situations?

5. Effective communication skills: Is the project manager able to operate as the focal point for communication with a variety of stakeholders?

It is important to note the commonalties across these studies and draw some general conclusions about the nature of project leadership.

- Effective project managers must be good communicators. Much of their time is spent in one form of communication or another. Whether they chair meetings, brainstorm solutions to problems, or maintain information flows with the client and upper management, effective project leaders are adept at all forms of communication.

- Project leaders must possess the flexibility to respond to uncertain or ambiguous situations with a minimum of stress. The nature of project management work is that it does not follow easily defined or recurring patterns. Each project is to some degree unique, and each problem the team faces has to be viewed as a new problem, requiring flexibility of response and creativity.

- Strong project leaders work well with and through their project teams. They are adept at getting the most out of their subordinates through providing an atmosphere of challenge and creativity. They have the ability to build and reinforce a cohesive team atmosphere, based on trust and enthusiasm, for success. They understand their role in creating an environment in which team members are able to motivate themselves to perform at levels of excellence. They encourage, are supportive of their teams, and utilize the various people skills necessary to help the team perform to its maximum.

■ Good project leaders are skilled at various influence tactics. Political influence is an essential part of the implementation process. Hence, effective project managers must become well schooled in the art of persuasion and influence.

Although examining the traits of successful leaders is valuable, it only presents part of the picture. One key to understanding leadership behavior is to focus on what leaders do, rather than who they are. It is dangerous and often imprecise to draw overly large generalizations from the personal psychology of acknowledged leaders in an effort to try to better understand what psychological forces makes them operate in the manners in which they do. The uncritical use of currently popular psychoanalytical theories to investigate leaders ignores the influence of their organizations and ingrained cultural expectations, which can heavily influence leadership behavior (Gronn 1993). In other words, we spend far too much time analyzing leaders after they become acknowledged leaders, instead of investigating the forces that originally shaped them. If it is more appropriate to examine leadership in terms of its behavior, let us therefore consider some of the more common demands made upon project managers and their approaches for responding to these demands.

The Dimensions of Information and Decision Authority

Let us imagine the manager of a five-person IS implementation team. She is faced with a problem that is complex; yet a decision must be made. From the standpoint of leadership, the project manager must answer two "predecision" questions (Slevin 1991; Blanchard and Zigarmi 1985):

1. Where do I get the information input? (Whom do I ask for relevant information?)

2. Where should I place the decision authority for this problem? (Who makes the decision?)

The first question asks which members of the project team will furnish information about a particular decision. The second asks to what extent the manager retains all decision-making authority, or to what extent is that manager willing to *share* decision authority with members of the team, allowing them to make the decision in a more or less democratic fashion.

The first dimension is one of source of information, the second, one of decision authority; both are critical dimensions essential for effective leadership. They have been plotted on the graph in Figure 8.1, the

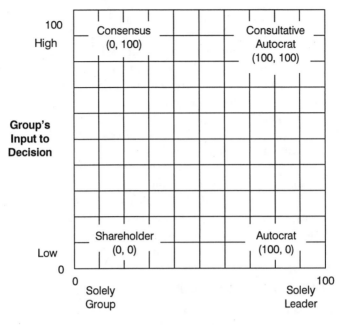

From Slevin and Pinto (1991)

Figure 8.1   The Bonoma/Slevin Leadership Model

Bonoma/Slevin Leadership Model. As leaders, managers may either request large amounts of subordinate information input into a decision or very small amounts; this is the vertical axis-information input. Secondly, leaders' decision-making styles may range from making a decision entirely by themselves to sharing their power with the group—the horizontal axis-decision authority.

Four Leadership Styles

Referring to Figure 8.1, it is possible to describe almost every leadership style (Slevin and Pinto 1988). The four extremes of leadership can be depicted in the four corners of the grid; they are characterized as follows.

■ Autocrat (100, 0): Such managers solicit little or no information from their project teams and make managerial decisions solely by themselves.

- Consultative Autocrat (100, 100): In this managerial style, intensive information input is elicited from the team members, but such formal leaders keep all substantive decision-making authority to themselves.
- Consensus (0, 100): Purely consensual managers throw open the problem to the group for discussion (information input), and simultaneously allow or encourage the entire group to make the relevant decision.
- Shareholder (0, 0): This position represents literally poor management. Little or no information input and exchange take place within the group context, while the group itself is provided ultimate authority for the final decision.

The advantages of the leadership model, apart from its practical simplicity, become more apparent when we consider three traditional aspects of leadership and managerial decision style: 1) participative management, 2) delegation, and, 3) pressures affecting leadership.

PARTICIPATIVE MANAGEMENT

The concept of participation in management is a complex one with different meanings for different individuals. In discussing the notion of participation with managers in a variety of settings, this is a typical response: "Oh, I participated with my subordinates on that decision. I asked each of them what they thought before I made the decision."

To many practicing managers, participation is often an informational concept, i.e., permitting sufficient subordinate input to be made before the hierarchical decision is handed down. On the other hand, when academics address the concept of participation, the following response is more often typically made: "Managers should use participation management more often. They should allow their subordinates to make the final decision with them in a consensual manner." To the academic, the concept of participation is usually an issue of power, i.e., moving to the left on the Bonoma/Slevin Model so that decision authority is shared with the group.

In actuality, participation is a two-dimensional construct. It involves both the solicitation of information and the sharing of power or decision authority. Neither dimension, in and of itself, is a sufficient indicator of a participative leadership style. Participative management requires equal emphasis on the project manager requesting information, allowing a more democratic decision-making dynamic to be adopted.

DELEGATION

Good project managers delegate effectively. In doing so, they negotiate some sort of compromise between the extreme of *abdication* (letting subordinates decide everything) and *autocratic management* (doing everything

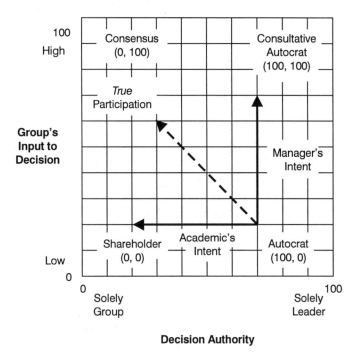

Decision Authority

From Slevin and Pinto (1991)

Figure 8.2   Bonoma/Slevin Model Showing Participative Decision-Making

themselves). The Bonoma/Slevin Leadership Model is useful as a learning device for managers as they delegate work to their subordinates. After exposure to the model, managers are often more explicit about the informational and decision-authority requirements of the delegated task. For example, the project manager might say to a subordinate: "Get the information that you need from my files and also check with Administration (information). Make the decision yourself (decision authority), but notify me in writing as soon as you have made it so that I am kept informed."

Thus, the subordinate understands both the information and decision-authority aspects of the delegated tasks. Delegation often fails when the communication is unclear on either or both of these dimensions (Leana 1986). To illustrate—there is a strong likelihood of difficulties occurring when managers phrase their instructions in such a way that subordinates are not clear about what information they are expected to provide and when it is needed, and how much power or discretion they possess to use their best judgment on the action to be taken.

Pressures Affecting Leadership

Implementation managers must learn that they may be required to act differently as a leader under different conditions, depending upon three kinds of pressure: 1) problem-attributes pressures, 2) leader-personality pressures, and, 3) organization/group pressures.

Think of the Bonoma/Slevin Leadership Model in terms of a map of the U.S.; Table 8.1 summarizes these pressures on leadership style in terms of geographical direction. (For example, a movement north is a movement upward on the vertical axis of the leadership model and so on.)

Problem-attributes pressures. Problem-attributes pressures generate eastward forces on the leader. In other words, they often cause leaders to take the sole majority or most of the decision-making authority upon themselves. This is especially true when problems are characterized as:

- time bound (a quick decision is required)
- important
- personal
- structured and routine.

In such cases, it is very tempting to take personal control over the decisional process to get the job done. This phenomenon is particularly apparent with managers new to the job or insecure about their status as a team member vis-à-vis their subordinates. They may not be inclined to trust subordinates to make either an accurate or timely decision, believing instead that one of the leader's prerogatives is to retain decision-making authority. However, northward pressures (involving the quest for additional information) can occur as well, given the importance of the decisions— decisions for which leaders lack the resources to make them themselves— and problems in which subordinate implementation is critical to success.

In these cases, information input and exchange will be maximized. Time pressures tend to push one toward the east, into an *autocratic mode*. Implementation concerns push one to the northwest, in search of both more information and active participation in and support of the decision by subordinates. It is a well-known behavioral finding that people cooperate more in implementing decisions that they have helped make.

Leader-personality pressures. Some managers tend to be inflexible in their leadership style, because of who they are and how they like to manage. For example, both past research and personal experience have led us to conclude that, in many cases, such managers have a high need for power, are task oriented, or are highly intelligent.

Managers of this type will make many decisions themselves that might otherwise be left to subordinates, and they may also make decisions without acquiring information from the group. People-oriented leaders, on the other hand, will act to maximize information inputs from their

Types of Pressure	Direction of Pressure on Leadership Grid
Problem-Attributes Pressures	
Leader lacks relevant information; problem is ambiguous.	North—more information needed.
Leader lacks enough time to make decision adequately.	South and east—consensus and information collection take time.
Decision is important or critical to leader.	North and east—personal control and information maximized.
Problem is structured or routine.	South and east—little time as possible spent on decision.
Decision implementation by subordinates is critical to success.	West and north—input and consensus required.
Leader-Personality Pressures	
Leader has high need for power.	East—personal control maximized.
Leader is high in need for affiliation; is *people oriented.*	North and west—contact with people maximized.
Leader is highly intelligent.	East—personal competence demonstrated.
Leader has high need for achievement.	East—personal contribution maximized.
Organizational and Group Pressures	
Conflict is likely to result from decision.	North and west—participative aspects of decision-making maximized.
Good leader-group relations exist.	North and west—group contact maximized.
Centrality is high or formalization of organization is high.	South and east—organization style is matched.

Table 8.2   Pressures on Leadership Style

subordinates and to share their decision authority as well. Both of these activities are people processes.

Project team leaders should perform some sort of self-assessment in terms of their preferred style for leading. It is often the case that project managers professing themselves frustrated with the intransigence or willful obstinacy of subordinates are simply illustrating that they and their subordinates have very different personality styles. Consequently, when leaders use an autocratic style because it suits their personality, they usually discover that this approach is exactly antithetical to the management style the subordinate needs in order to function effectively. Until project managers do a better job of assessing their own preferred leadership styles, they will in essence be operating with one eye deliberately kept closed to the considerations and needs of team members. Personality preferences do not simply represent a predilection on the project leader's part; they offer the potential threat of very damaging biases.

Organizational/group pressures. If conflict is likely to result from any decision made, effective managers are most likely to want their subordinates as involved as possible in both the input (northward) and authority (westward) dimensions, to help manage potential conflict. Should good leader/group relations exist, pressure northward (but not necessarily westward) will be felt. The leader will feel great pressure to fit into the *culture* of the organization. The R&D lab expects a consensual approach; most business groups expect a consultative autocrat approach; the factory floor may expect an autocratic approach. It is important to match your style to the norms, needs, and expectations of your subordinates.

The key is flexibility. No one leadership style is best for all situations. Rather, the successful manager is flexible and moves around the model as appropriate for the given situation. If time pressures are overwhelming, autocratic decision-making may be appropriate. For a majority of management decision-making, the consultative-autocratic approach may be the best alternative. And, in dealing with high-tech professionals, engineers, and other specialists, the project manager may choose a more consensual style. The key to success for project managers is to match leadership style to the situation.

Some Observations on Project Management Leadership Styles

Based on the presentation and discussion of this leadership model with literally hundreds of practicing managers, some conclusions concerning project manager leadership styles have been derived.

You Are More Autocratic Than You Think

In the eyes of subordinates, most managers are probably closer to the autocrat leadership style than they perceive themselves to be. Why? The answer is because the manager is the boss of the subordinates. Managers often have an idealized vision of their leadership styles. These leaders are not trying to fraudulently claim a style that is not theirs. They may truly believe that they are consensus managers who actively solicit information from subordinates and involve them in the decision process. Unfortunately, subordinates rarely see it that way. No matter how easygoing, friendly, participative, and supportive managers are, they are still *the boss*. There is almost always a difference in leadership style as perceived by supervisors and subordinates.

But It May Be O.K.

Often, when subordinates are asked in which direction they would like their boss to move on the graph, they respond, "Things are O.K. as they are." Even though there are perceptual discrepancies concerning leadership style, there may not necessarily be a felt need or pressure for change; the status quo may be acceptable. In some situations, subordinates truly desire more freedom and autonomy in decision-making. However, in other cases, although the rhetoric of decision-making freedom is employed, when directly offered autonomy, subordinates prove to be more comfortable allowing the boss to shoulder the responsibility for decision-making. There is no hard and fast rule here. Leaders need to address the personalities of their own subordinates, and develop and encourage those who are willing to take on decision-making responsibilities. Often, those individuals are the future leaders in the organization.

It Is Easy to Move North and South

It tends to be much easier to move vertically on the graph, because management is a job of communication. It is easy to collect more information or less information from subordinates before making a decision. Even if the intent of the manager is not to make use of the information that is collected, it is easy to ask for or not ask for input from subordinates. The information dimension is the least resistant to change.

It Is Difficult to Move West

As opposed to the dimension of information, most managers find it quite threatening to move westward too quickly. *West* implies the willingness to give up some decision authority to the group. The primary reason for most managers' hesitation is that a westward movement upsets the basic power realities in the organization. Willingly foregoing the power prerogatives that are a part of a manager's position is a difficult adjustment for most of us to make. Further, if the manager is under severe time pressure, if the decision is of major importance, or if problems are continually besetting the implementation effort, it is very difficult to turn the decision-making process over to subordinates. The point is that there may be a thousand seemingly legitimate excuses for refusing to involve subordinates in decision-making. Project managers need to examine these reasons as objectively as they can, to determine if reluctance is based on appropriate reasons or other, more personal ones.

IF SUBORDINATES' EXPECTATIONS ARE NOT MET, MORALE WILL SUFFER

Team members often have expectations about the decision-making and leadership style of the project manager. Based on past experiences and beliefs about how a leader should act, they become comfortable with certain styles. Therefore, if the project manager does not employ the expected style, it can have a detrimental effect on morale. For example, if subordinates are expecting their leader to use a consensual style, and the leader prefers an autocratic decision-making style, subordinate morale is likely to decline. Interestingly, the reverse case is also often true. When subordinates are accustomed to and expect their manager to make all decisions in an autocratic style, they can become very uncomfortable when confronted with a manager who prefers group decision-making. They are simply not used to being asked for their opinions, and hence, once again, morale may decline. The essential point here is that the decision process can be as important as the decision outcome, especially from the standpoint of motivating subordinates.

BE FLEXIBLE

Successful managers are autocratic when they need to be, consultative when necessary, and consensual when the situation calls for it. It is possible and indeed desirable to move around the leadership space to fit the needs of the situation. Unsuccessful managers are inflexible and try the same style in all situations. Experienced consultants often discover—when asking these managers why they do not adopt more flexible leadership styles—that managers tend to be very resistant to recognizing they have options. Yet, they can develop flexibility in their approach to practices such as delegation and participatory decision-making.

Using Alternative Leadership Styles

The leadership framework presented in the Bonoma/Slevin Model requires the manager to ask two key questions concerning decision-making:

1. Who do I ask?
2. Who makes the decision?

The manager's ability to obtain accurate information input from subordinates is crucial to effective IS implementation. Similarly, decision-making authority must be located in the right place vis-à-vis the leader's group. This model can also be applied more broadly to system implementation in general.

Information systems are successfully implemented through sufficient access to and judicious use of both information and power. At the start of any implementation effort, the implementation team leader might be well advised to review the status of project information and power. Among the key questions that must be considered are issues such the following.

- Who or what will serve as the primary source(s) of information for this implementation?
- Does the team have access to accurate and plentiful information from all relevant stakeholders?
- Who has the power to make decisions and get those decisions implemented?

These and other questions form the basis for determining the viability of the leader's various options for decision-making. Unless the members of the team have access to and are able to collect necessary information, a consensual leadership style will be wasted. It does no good to ask uninformed sources their opinions. Likewise, do team leaders in this company have the authority (given the organization's culture and norms) to give up some of their decision-making authority, or are they expected to make all decisions by themselves?

These questions are appropriate, and they establish the fundamental basis of decision-making: Project managers must become aware of and comfortable with various leadership styles and use them as necessary in decision-making situations. Making use of the Bonoma/Slevin Model and understanding the nature of leadership can help project managers more effectively manage their projects, while at the same time facilitating professional development of subordinates and maintaining high levels of team morale.

9

Implementation Champions: Our Most Valuable Untapped Resource

Developing and implementing new innovations such as information systems (IS) in organizations has long been acknowledged as a difficult and time-consuming task. In an effort to reduce the complexities inherent in IS implementation, project managers and those tasked with the job of implementing these new systems are constantly in search of new methods, management techniques, and organizational issues to address. So far, we have examined a number of the relevant organizational and managerial issues for more effective adoption of IS technologies, including understanding politics, managing team building, developing comprehensive planning activities, and so on. One issue that has also had a significant impact on many successful implementation efforts, and yet has been rarely articulated, is the role champions play in IS adoption success.

This chapter demonstrates the importance a champion can have in successful IS implementation. The types of organizational members who frequently take on the role of champion are identified, as well as the types of duties they are called upon to perform. Finally, given a better understanding of how champions function in organizations, some guidelines for developing and encouraging the proliferation of champions throughout both public and private organizations are provided.

The existence of champions has long been recognized both in the organizational theory literature and within organizations themselves. While there are a number of definitions of champions and their unique activities, all possessing relatively similar characteristics, one of the earliest definitions is perhaps the best. A champion is defined as an individual who:

> identifies with a new development (whether or not he made it), using all the weapons at his command, against the funded resistance of the organization. He functions as an entrepreneur within the organization, and since he does not have official authority to take unnecessary risks ... he puts his job in the organization (and often his standing ...) on the line. ... He (has) great energy and capacity to invite and withstand disapproval. (Schon 1967).

Champions possess some remarkable characteristics. First, it is assumed (in fact, it seems almost expected) that champions will be operating without the officially sanctioned approval of their organizations. Oftentimes, they set themselves directly at odds with the established order or popular way of thinking. Standard operating procedures are anathema to champions, and they are usually unafraid of bringing official disapproval down upon themselves. Second, champions have a true entrepreneurial talent for recognizing value in innovative ideas or products, which too often escapes the typical organizational member. Third, perhaps because of this entrepreneurial streak, champions have a high threshold for job insecurity. Put another way, champions are risk takers in every sense of the word. Their single-minded pursuit of truth in whatever innovative form it may take often puts them at odds with entrenched bureaucrats and those who do not share their enthusiasm for a new product or idea.

Based on our own experiences with these individuals, we would like to offer a generalized definition of champions. A champion is a person within the organization who is entrepreneurial with power. In other words, champions must use their power within the organization in an entrepreneurial manner. Recent articles defined the characteristics of entrepreneurial activity, arguing that entrepreneurs are individuals willing to take risks, be proactive, and strive for innovation, or constant improvement (Covin and Slevin 1988; Slevin and Covin 1990). Champions, too, must be willing to use both their personal power and the power of their position to proactively search for opportunities and threats, encourage innovation, and, perhaps most importantly, be willing to put their careers on the line and take risks to support the innovations they champion.

It is difficult to truly capture the enthusiasm and fervor that champions have for their ideas. Peters, best-selling author of *In Search of Excellence*, describes champions as "fanatics" in their single-minded pursuit of their pet ideas. He goes further to state that, "the people who are tenacious, committed champions are often a royal pain in the neck. … They must be fostered and nurtured—even when it hurts" (1985). In this statement, Peters captures the essence of the personality and impact of the champion: one who is both an organizational gadfly and, at the same time, vitally important for project and organizational success.

Champions—Who Are They?

One of the intriguing characteristics of champions is that these individuals do not consistently occupy the same positions within the organization. While we often find senior managers serving as champions, many members of the organization can play the role of implementation champion with different systems or at different times with the same system implementation project. Among the specific and most common types of champions are the following (Meredith 1986):

- creative originator—an engineer, city planner, scientist, or similar person who is the source of and driving force behind an idea
- entrepreneur—the person who adopts the idea or technology and actively works to sell the system throughout the organization, eventually pushing it to success
- "Godfather" or sponsor—a senior-level manager who does everything possible to promote the project including obtaining the needed resources, coaching the implementation team when problems arise, calming the political waters, and protecting the implementation effort when necessary
- manager of the implementation effort—the administrator or project manager who handles the operational planning and day-to-day details.

CREATIVE ORIGINATOR

In a sense, the notion that the individual who was behind the original development of the idea or technology can function as the implementation champion is hardly surprising. No one in the organization has more expertise or sense of vision where the new IS is concerned. Few others possess the technical or creative ability to develop the implementation effort through to fruition. Consequently, many organizations allow, and even actively encourage, the continued involvement of the scientist or engineer who originally developed the idea upon which the project is based. Not only are creative originators excellent cheerleaders and aggressive project developers, but they are also handy troubleshooters to be used when problems develop within the implementation effort.

Because IS technology is generally adequately developed and well accepted in the marketplace, the role of a creative originator in introducing IS technology to an organization will tend to be different from that of an in-house champion responsible for a company developing a new product on its own. In this sense, the creative originator may simply be a technically proficient manager who recognizes the value of IS technology that already exists in the marketplace and agitates for its adoption within the organization. Typically, the creative originator's role is that of IS advocate. Perhaps these champions were originally employed by other organizations that made use of an IS, or they became converts through witnessing demonstrations of the technology at professional meetings or trade shows. The important point is that these champions become truly enthused about the possibilities presented to their organizations in adopting IS technology. Consequently, they often become organizations' most aggressive advocates of the system.

ENTREPRENEUR

In many organizations, it is not possible, for a variety of constraining reasons, for the creative originator or original IS advocate to assume the role of the implementation champion. Often, the scientist, technician, and/or engineer are limited by the need to perform the specifically demarcated duties of their positions, thereby precluding them from becoming part of the project-implementation team. In situations such as these, the individual who often steps forward as the implementation champion is someone referred to as an *organizational entrepreneur*. The entrepreneur is an organizational member who recognizes the value of the original idea or technology, and makes it a personal goal to gain its acceptance throughout the relevant organizational units that would be employing it. Entrepreneurial champions are usually middle-to-upper level managers, who may or may not have technical backgrounds. In addition to performing their own duties within the organization, they are constantly on the lookout for new, innovative, and useful ideas to develop.

Just as the name implies, the entrepreneur is a high-energy individual working to make others realize the exciting potential of the new information technology. His primary role within the organization is attempting to sell the idea to upper management-personnel that can aid in the project's acquisition and internal acceptance. Even though entrepreneurs are not the creative, originating forces behind ideas, they often play the role of visionary or head cheerleader for the implementation team, as well as for as the rest of the organization.

GODFATHER OR SPONSOR

The implementation champion as godfather is a role often played by a member of the senior-management team in the organization. This person has elected to actively support acquisition and implementation of the new technology, and do everything in her power to facilitate this process. One of the most important functions of godfathers is to make it known throughout the organization that this implementation effort is under their personal guidance or protection. In addition to supplying this *protection*, the godfather engages in a variety of activities of a more substantial nature to help the implementation effort succeed. She makes certain that resources will remain available to the project team throughout the development and implementation process. Consequently, the project team can perform its work without having to worry about whether or not funding for the new technology will be withdrawn or cut back before completion of the implementation process.

In addition to providing and ensuring the continued supply of necessary resources for the system implementation, a godfather can also use her influence to coach the team when problems arise in order to decrease the likelihood of political problems derailing the project. Because the implementation effort is under the protection of the godfather, one important service provided is addressing and forestalling likely problems, of either an operational or political nature, from devolving onto the project team. The godfather is sponsoring the new system. Therefore, she is likely to do everything possible to smooth potential difficulties throughout the acquisition and implementation stages, not only in terms of ensuring continuous supplies of a variety of resources, but also through exerting considerable political influence within the organization acquiring the new system.

PROJECT MANAGER

The final member of the organization who may play the role of implementation champion is the project manager. At one time or another, almost every project manager has undertaken the duties of champion. The task of the leader of the implementation process is exceedingly complex, requiring one to be administrator, cheerleader, ambassador, integrator, and planner (Stuckenbruck 1978). In addition to the many official duties expected of project managers, there is a wide variety of unofficial activities in which the head of the implementation team must engage to successfully implement the prospective IS. Project champion is often one of the unofficial roles. When one considers the definition of implementation champion and the wide range of duties performed, it becomes clear why the manager of the implementation effort is often in the best position to engage in championing behaviors. Certainly, this individual is strongly identified with the system, and, to a degree, his career is directly tied to the successful acquisition and implementation of the IS.

Although implementation team leaders should be the logical choice for the individual to function as champion, there are some compelling reasons why many project managers do not take the role. For example, many project managers, in trying to maintain the role of project champion, become so caught up in the day-to-day details and activities of their projects that they are unable to *shift gears* and develop a more general organizationwide view. In other cases, project leaders are technical specialists more comfortable paying attention to details than with focusing on the larger, corporatewide picture. After spending the week involved in the more micro-operational activities of implementation, these leaders often find it exceedingly difficult to assess the project from the larger perspective of how it fits into the current goals and realities of the organization.

Further, the political realities of the organization may make it impossible for the project manager to function jointly as implementer of the system and as its champion. Either the project manager may lack some necessary political connections or be loath to engage in organizational politicking. Additionally, in many organizations, the head of the implementation effort is simply not high enough within the organizational hierarchy to be in a position to ensure a continued supply of resources. In either case, the system's implementation would be greatly aided by the support of a member of the organization external to but actively cooperating with the implementation team.

The Functions of A Champion

One study sought to identify the different activities associated with champions when aiding in the implementation process (J. K. Pinto and Slevin 1988b). Fifty-one project managers were asked to think of a project in which they could identify an individual (or individuals) who acted as project champion. They were further asked to identify that individual's position within the organization, and make a list of the variety of activities in which the champion engaged. Table 9.1 lists the set of championing activities identified by the study's sample of project managers.

The organizational roles of champions closely parallel the four categories previously listed: 1) creative originator, 2) entrepreneur, 3) god-

Role	Number	Percentage
Creative Originator	13	25
Entrepreneur	11	22
Godfather	20	39
Project Manager	7	14

Table 9.1   Champions as Identified by the Roles They Undertook on the Project

father, and, 4) project manager. Of these fifty-one projects, godfather was the most frequently recognized role.

Table 9.2 shows that the major, identified activities in which these champions engaged, while ten in number, fell into two basic categories. For the purposes of this chapter, we have termed the two types of championing duties as *traditional* and *nontraditional* sides of implementation management.

The first set of activities in Table 9.2 is commonly thought to represent the traditional duties of managers. The champion can actively aid in the IS implementation process by interpreting technical details, providing strong leadership, and helping with project coordination and control, as well as supplying administrative help for the implementation team. It is important that the champion is familiar with the technical aspects of the system. A champion who does not understand the basic technological issues involved in the system being implemented will not help, and actually may hurt, the system's chances for successful implementation. Another important traditional activity of the project champion is in procurement of necessary resources to enable team members to perform their tasks. Champions are often in an excellent position to make available a continual supply of logistical support for the implementation team.

The second set of activities in which the champion will engage is classified in Table 9.2 as the nontraditional side of management. We use the term advisedly, implying that these are not the usual roles identified in traditional management literature. We do not mean to imply that these activities are in any way unnecessary or eccentric. Rather, as several interviewed champions have related, these duties are equally important for implementation success as the more frequently identified, well-known

Traditional

1. **Technical Understanding:** Knowledge of the technical aspects involved in developing and implementing the system.

2. **Leadership and Team Building:** The ability to provide leadership and motivation for the implementation team.

3. **Coordination and Control:** Managing and controlling the activities of the team.

4. **Obtain and Provide Support:** Gaining access to the necessary resources (financial, human, and logistical) to ensure a smooth implementation process.

5. **Administrative:** Handling the important administrative side of the system's adoption (e.g., paper work, scheduling, allocating, and so on).

Nontraditional

1. **Cheerleader:** Proving the needed motivation (spiritual driving force) for the team.

2. **Visionary:** Maintaining a clear sense of purpose and a firm idea of what is involved in adopting the new system.

3. **Politician:** Playing the necessary political games and maintaining the important contacts to ensure broad-based acceptance of the information system on the part of the other impacted units in the organization.

4. **Risk Taker:** Being willing to take calculated personal or career risks to bring the system online.

5. **Ambassador:** Maintaining good contacts with the three groups external to and affecting the system's implementation success (intended users, top management, and the rest of the impacted organization).

Table 9.2   The Traditional and Nontraditional Sides of Champion Behavior

requirements for successful management. Performing functions such as cheerleader, visionary, politician, risk taker, ambassador, and so forth are intuitively important for most managers, yet they tend to be de-emphasized in the literature, job specifications, and training programs for IS managers. As one champion put it, "We can teach people those (traditional) skills easily enough, but experience is the best teacher for the other (non-traditional) duties. *No one prepares you for the irrational side of this job. You have to pick it up as you go*" (emphasis added).

One of the unique aspects of champions is that in many organizations the majority of their time is not engaged in performing the traditional side of implementation-management duties, but rather in these nontraditional activities. The champion is often the person with the vision, the cheerleader, or the driving force behind the implementation effort. Additionally, the champion is expected to take on key political roles in attempting to play the right kinds of games, make the right contacts, and network with the necessary people to ensure a steady supply of resources necessary for the implementation effort to succeed. Finally, because by definition champions strongly identify with the new system, much of their time is spent in networking with other organizational units, top management, and prospective clients (users) of the system. As such, they take on an important ambassador/advocate role throughout the organization. In many cases, champions put their careers on the line to support and gain acceptance of the new system and, as a result, become committed to aiding the implementation effort in every way possible, through both traditional and nontraditional activities.

Figure 9.1 illustrates the distinction we draw between project managers and system champions, through their involvement in the traditional and nontraditional aspects of their duties. In general, we find that project managers, because of their concern for the daily, micro-aspects of the implementation effort, tend to focus their power and energy on the traditional side of the management process. It is not that project managers are intrinsically uncomfortable with the nontraditional side of implementation management, but that the traditional activities are often more visible, or seem more pressing, and often consume the vast majority of a project manager's time.

Champions, on the other hand, typically rely on the nontraditional side of power and management style in helping to successfully implement an IS. Because champions' roles include those of creative originator, entrepreneur, or godfather, they may have little power to actively influence the rational side of the implementation process, focusing instead upon the irrational activities of risk taking, cheerleading, being ambassador, and others.

Does Championing Behavior Matter?

One question that is often asked is whether or not this type of behavior really plays an important role in the successful implementation of new

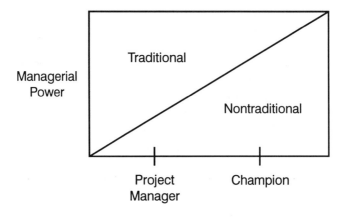

Figure 9.1   The Project Manager and Champion's Uses of Traditional and Nontraditional Power

information systems. The answer to this question is an emphatic "yes." Aside from anecdotal and case-study information (Maidique 1980), there are also some compelling research studies that have helped us better understand not only what champions do, but how important champions are for acquiring and gaining organizational acceptance of innovative IS.

Two studies in particular have gone a long way toward making the case for the importance of champions in implementation. One, conducted almost twenty years ago, examined a series of new product developments and start-ups at a variety of organizations (Chakrabarti 1974). Their relationship to the presence or absence of an identifiable organizational champion was studied on forty-five new product development efforts (both successful and unsuccessful). Of the seventeen successful new product developments, all but one, or 94 percent, had a readily identifiable champion. That is, an individual to whom the majority of those involved in the project could point and identify as the project's sponsor or champion spearheaded these ventures. On the other hand, of the twenty-eight projects that failed, only one was coupled with an identifiable development champion. Clearly, the results of this study point to the enormously important role that a champion can play in new-product development.

The second study examined the impact of champions on new IS acquisition and adoption (Onsrud and J. K. Pinto 1993). A sample of over two hundred municipalities and small-town governments that had recently acquired IS technology was sampled. One of the questions asked was to assess the importance of the presence of a visible and identifiable in-house champion for the acquisition and eventual adoption of the IS. On a five-point scale, with endpoints labeled "Not at all important" to "Extremely important," the sample rated the importance of a champion at 4.45—clearly an indication of the degree of importance afforded most champions in organizations intent on introducing new technologies.

These two examples demonstrate empirical support for a phenomenon that is well known and accepted within most organizations, as evidenced by the significant amount of anecdotal evidence, case studies, and war stories that are cited at professional conferences and in the relevant journals. The process of championing does matter. It can have a significant positive effect on implementing new or innovative systems within an organization, and it can greatly reduce the concomitant anxiety and uncertainty toward the newly acquired IS.

The Championing Process

Because so much research to date has pointed to the impact of championing behavior, many organizations are not willing to simply sit back and hope that a champion will emerge to help manage the implementation process. Such organizations have taken a more direct approach. When a new project or system is in the process of being acquired and implemented, if a project champion does not step forward, someone from the upper-management ranks will be appointed to carry out the duties of a champion. It is true that a self-appointed champion will invariably be able to generate more enthusiasm and take more risks for the newly acquired system; however, these organizations believe that, properly trained in their responsibilities, a variety of people from top management are able to function effectively as champions.

A recent example of a successful new computerized system implementation illustrates the importance of the project-championing role. A medium-sized manufacturing firm initiated a project to install a comprehensive computer-aided design and manufacturing (CAD/CAM) system for its shop-floor operations. It was predicted that successful development of this new system would reduce front-end production time and costs by almost 15 percent. The creative originator (a senior production engineer) filled the original champion role. He effectively lobbied throughout the upper echelons of the organization for the innovation, and then worked throughout the conceptualization and planning stages for its implementation, to eliminate objections, budgetary roadblocks, and scheduling conflicts. While originally viewed as somewhat of a nuisance, his single-minded energy eventually won enough support to initiate predevelopment studies and, eventually, system-development funding. Once the project was under way, the vice president of manufacturing, who by now had perceived the many benefits of successful implementation, assumed the championing role. In effect, he took over the championing role as the system's godfather. His primary contribution to the project came in the form of smoothing the political side of the implementation effort and ensuring continued funding, even in the midst of an economic downturn. Further, he enlisted support for the new system from the engineering department, probably the next most important group of eventual users of the CAD/CAM system.

Although the system is just beginning to go online, the early returns have been extremely encouraging. In the departments where the CAD/CAM system has been installed, it has been widely used and has already led to cost savings. Initial front-end manufacturing savings projections of 15 percent have already been revised upward to 20 percent. When questioned about the reasons for the success of this new system, individuals from a variety of functional departments pointed to the part played by the creative originator (engineer) and godfather (vice president of manufacturing) in providing an excellent environment for the system to be successfully developed and implemented.

A second example of the impact of championing recently occurred in an IS introduction within the planning department of a major northeastern United States city. In this example, the role of champion was played by a creative originator (planning engineer), who witnessed demonstrations of IS technology at a recent professional meeting. He became so enthused with the potential uses for the new technology that he began a one-person advertising and promotional campaign within his department. He initiated feasibility studies, contacted possible vendors to arrange for site demonstrations and pilot projects, and served as a vocal advocate for the system within budgeting meetings.

It was largely through his energetic efforts that the city council eventually granted funding for the IS and its use within a number of city departments including planning, tax assessment, public works, public safety, and residential and urban redevelopment. This champion's duties did not stop with the city simply acquiring the new technology; he spent a significant amount of time arranging training sessions for all impacted individuals and departments and set up a hotline through his office for handling technical problems with the system. During our interviews, conducted over two years after its implementation, planners and other affected personnel were almost unanimous in their praise of the new system, remembering with amusement the old days when they "had to use paper maps."

This example has an interesting note in that the individual who was almost single-handedly responsible for the acquisition and adoption of IS technology left the city planning office approximately eighteen months after the system was introduced. He is currently employed as county planner for a large county in the northeast United States where, at last report, he was actively involved in pushing for its adoption and use of an IS!

Guidelines for Developing Champions

It is important to understand that all organizations (both public and private) differ in terms of availability of individuals to take on the role of a system champion. Although some organizations have a supply of enthusiastic personnel at all levels willing to serve as champions, the reality for most organizations is not nearly so upbeat. The fault, in this case, is not that these organizations have inadequate or unskilled people. Very often, the problem is the organizations have failed to recognize the benefits to be derived from champions. Champions and a climate in which they can exist must be developed and nurtured by the organization. Following are some general guidelines for organizations to use to gain the full benefits from innovation champions.

IDENTIFY AND ENCOURAGE THE EMERGENCE OF CHAMPIONS

It is paramount that organizations create an atmosphere in which champions can develop. Companies and public agencies must work to create a climate that is conducive to the championing process. To illustrate, consider the examples of the CAD/CAM and city IS implementations. In many organizations, a creative originator who continually badgered upper management for a new product or system would likely offend some members of the key top-management team. The result would either be some form of disciplinary action or, at the very least, a *gag order* placed on the originator to ensure that this person did not further trouble upper management. As you can imagine, such action would result in no one else in that organization ever putting his neck out. If this is the way innovative ideas are rewarded, why should anyone even bother?

ENCOURAGE AND REWARD RISK TAKERS

Jack Welch, chief executive officer of General Electric, has made it a personal crusade to actively encourage senior, middle, and even junior managers to take risks. His argument has been that innovation does not come without risk; if one cannot bear to take risks, one cannot innovate. In the same sense, implementation champions are classic examples of risk takers. In many cases, they put their prestige, reputations, and careers on the line in the single-minded pursuit of an idea in which they believe.

The corollary to encouraging and rewarding risk takers is to avoid the knee-jerk response of punishing those involved in failed implementation efforts. In many organizations, project managers who are successful are rewarded, while individuals who manage projects that fail are deemed unsuccessful or are even punished. Innovative systems are, by definition, risky ventures. They can result in tremendous payoffs, but they also have a very real possibility of failure. Organizations have to become more aware of the positive effects of encouraging individuals to take risks, and assume championing roles in innovative system implementations such as IS. Even in cases when the project fails, it is important to recognize the efforts of the project team and champion. As Welch has said, one project success can often pay for ten project failures. Risk takers and champions must be rewarded for their efforts, whatever the outcome.

DO NOT TIE CHAMPIONS TOO TIGHTLY TO THE TRADITIONAL SIDE OF MANAGEMENT

With the exception of project managers, the roles played by champions (creative originator, entrepreneur, and godfather) are often more conducive to the nontraditional side of management. Champions, by definition, use their power in an entrepreneurial manner. Because they tend to be visionaries, cheerleaders, and risk takers, they approach their goals with single-minded strength of purpose and a sense of the overall design and strategy for the new technology. Many times, a champion has little taste for the more routine or mundane aspects of system acquisition and implementation such as planning and scheduling, allocating resources, and handling the administrative details. Their expertise and true value to the implementation process may be in their political connections and contributions—in employing the nontraditional side of power. As a result, it is less common to see project managers functioning in the dual roles of manager of the micro-aspects of the implementation and more general system champion. In particular, organizations that assign champions on a project-by-project basis almost invariably choose a member of upper management who is adept at the nontraditional side of the system-implementation process.

If Necessary, Use Multiple Champions

A final point that needs to be underscored is the observation that it is often not only possible but appropriate to have multiple champions emerge for a single system's implementation. Using the aforementioned CAD/CAM project to illustrate, the initial champion was the creative originator, who originally conceived of the idea for the project and led the early push for system development. Later, during the project's full development and implementation, a senior executive effectively took over the championing role as the system's godfather or sponsor. It was during these later stages that the vice president was more effective at removing potential roadblocks, identifying and ensuring the support of system users, and overseeing the coordination among the departments involved in the implementation process. In essence, the two champions were effective in assisting in system development and implementation, but differentially so, at the distinct points in the process they were needed.

It may be that many system implementation efforts require only a single champion in order to be successfully introduced. For example, if the project manager is also fulfilling the role of champion, she is in an excellent position to oversee the IS from its needs-assessment determination through to its acquisition and implementation. However, due to most organizational realities—as well as the increasingly complex world in which organizations operate—it is often beneficial to make use of a variety of champions to play the different roles required for implementation success. New or highly innovative systems, in particular, may derive the most benefit from the availability of multiple champions across the introduction life cycle.

Conclusions

It is clear that the movement in IS introduction in the future is going to be toward increasing complexity and the demands for greater degrees of technical innovation. Both empirical research and anecdotal evidence have long supported the importance of the champion for successful new system implementation. This chapter presents in detail some of the specific characteristics of implementation champions: who they are, what they do, what impact they have on adoption success, and how organizations can develop them more effectively. Between sharing stories at conferences and reading the literature on IS, it seems increasingly clear that one element shared by many of today's successful system introductions is the presence of an acknowledged champion. Because the status of champions will continue to grow in our organizations in both the public and private sectors, it is important that champions be used in a more systematic manner to increase the chances of project success.

The End Game: Finishing the Project on a High Note

Better is the end of things than the beginning thereof.

Ecclesiastes 7: 8

Nothing is ended with honor that does not conclude better than it began.

Samuel Johnson

A long-held but implicit assumption of many project managers suggests that if the implementation process has been well managed, then the project is destined for success. This belief argues, in effect, that if the system comes in on budget and schedule and the product works, it will be readily accepted by its intended users; consequently, everyone will be satisfied. The reality is often less promising. Numerous companies and project managers can tell stories of projects that were well managed and cost effective, and yet the systems have never lived up to their potential because of a lack of acceptance on the part of their intended users.

Why should we foster this concern for the client? Rather than require information-system managers to accept as an article of faith the importance of considering the needs of users, let us examine some of the compelling reasons for including client acceptance in any equation for implementation success.

One reason for considering client needs has to do with the nature of many of today's information systems (IS). In today's competitive and increasingly international marketplace, we are faced with shortened product life cycles and rapidly increasing product obsolescence. Not only must systems be developed more rapidly, but also vendors are often required to devote considerable time to convincing prospective clients of the value of their product as compared to other commensurate alternatives. Increasingly, IS managers are called upon to act as liaison between the implementation team and the client, listening to needs and explaining how the project can address them (Takeuchi and Nonaka 1986).

A second reason for considering the needs of the user—one that is closely related to the first issue—concerns the often-detached nature of project teams within organizations. Many organizations so completely insulate their project teams that the team members have little awareness of not only the needs of the client, but also of other alternative products that are being introduced in direct competition with their systems (Souder 1988). This point was recently brought home to the authors at a project-training program attended by a variety of managers from both the marketing and R&D functions within a large organization. When we suggested the importance of considering the needs of the client in new project development, the entire marketing contingent applauded! As one marketer put it:

> We have been telling the engineers and R&D types for years that a project is only as good as it will sell. They seem to feel that if they can get it out the door on time and it works, it is destined for greatness. They refuse to understand that the client determines whether a product succeeds or fails.

A final reason for considering the needs of the client is suggested by the results of some recently conducted research (see Chapter 4) into the causes of project success or failure. J. K. Pinto and Slevin identified ten factors that are critical to the success or failure of projects (1988a). Two of the ten factors involve determining the needs of intended users: client consultation and client acceptance. Note the inclusion of a separate factor dealing with client acceptance. As the research demonstrates, it is not enough that project managers consult with clients early in the project's development to learn their special requirements and needs. Project teams must also take steps to create and initiate a program for *marketing* the system to its intended users once it has been developed.

Clearly, the function of marketing is becoming increasingly important for project teams and organizations. What is missing in implementation theory and practice, however, is a systematic understanding of the process by which products of projects are accepted and used. Further, we need to come to a far greater awareness of the role of IS managers and implementation team members in facilitating this acceptance. Managers need to understand that, in order to successfully introduce a system, they must assume a set of responsibilities and activities related to effectively *selling* the project to its clients. In essence, we need to transfer the IS manager's role into that of a marketer. One of the hard truths to which many IS managers can point, having learned it the hard way, is that sometimes system *success* has less to do with how the development process was managed, and more to do with how well the clients were convinced of the benefits or usefulness of the finished product.

The purpose of this chapter is to spell out, in some detail, the role of the IS team leader as marketer. Although some project managers readily understand and assume their responsibilities for aiding project acceptance, there are a large number of project managers who are either unaware of these marketing requirements or unsure of the steps involved in helping to sell the product of the project to its users. Our goal is to offer a project-marketing framework to help managers develop and focus their efforts toward successfully selling IS. This chapter suggests relevant steps in developing a project-marketing plan and offers guidelines and practical suggestions for teams to effectively address their *hidden responsibilities*.

The Information System Implementation Marketing-Plan Components

The marketing plan is a technique developed by marketers for plotting the strategy behind successful marketing and introduction of new products (Kotler 1980). For our purposes, we have taken the framework of a marketing plan and applied it to the roles and activities that project teams need to address in gaining client acceptance—that is, in successfully implementing IS technology. This segment addresses the specific sections of the project-marketing plan and suggests that managers need to develop plans, in the early stages of IS implementation, designed to sell the product of their efforts to the intended users.

Note: Although the following example of an IS marketing plan will sometimes use a new system-introduction project for illustrative purposes, these same basic principles can be applied to a variety of projects, both internal to the organization and intended for outside customers.

Projects undertaken for internal organization use still require considerable time and effort in assessing the needs of the intended clients. One of the common mistakes made by many IS managers is assuming that because the client is another department or unit within the same company, problems of acceptance and use will be minimal. This assumption is often false. Many of us are familiar with a number of projects that have consumed large amounts of time and money, and the results have never been used by other departments because we did not take the time to explain the project and ask them for their input and specific needs.

An overview of a project marketing plan is shown in Table 10.1. The various sections of the plan are detailed in the following sections.

CLIENT ANALYSIS

A client analysis is performed in order to gather information that will give the project team a sense of whether or not the client departments can and will accept and/or implement the system. The importance of an accurate and thorough client analysis has long been acknowledged as critical to the marketing function. Bower and Garda, for example, have argued that identifying customer requirements is essential to successful marketing (1986). Similarly, the key requirement for an adequate client analysis is open and ongoing interaction with the client. Only through such interaction will the project team acquire the knowledge needed to ensure that the system is acceptable from the client's point of view. A thorough client analysis will typically require assessment of at least six issue areas. These and some potentially relevant questions regarding each follow.

- Client's needs
  - What client needs will the system satisfy?
  - How critical to the client organization's effectiveness is the satisfaction of these needs?
  - Will transference of the as-ordered system enable the client to satisfy its needs?
  - Is there any reason to believe that what the client thinks it needs from the system is different from what it actually needs from the IS?
- Client's options/alternatives
  - Can the client's organization continue to operate effectively without the system?
  - Are there competing systems that the client may find equally acceptable?
  - Is the client fully aware of alternative means of satisfying the needs for which the IS was ordered?
  - What are the likely consequences for the client if it does not commit itself to the IS?
- Client's ability to influence project design parameters
  - How much influence does the client have, and how much does it want, over specific design specifications of the project?

I. **Client Analysis**

  a. Client's Needs

  b. Client's Options and Alternatives

  c. Client's Ability to Influence Design or Specifications

  d. Client's Tolerance Levels

    i. Cost

    ii. Time

    iii. Performance Specifications

  e. Client's Ability to Accept Transference

  f. Political Support

II. **Marketing Strategy**

  a. Marketing Objectives

  b. Marketing Mix

    i. Product

    ii. Promotion

    iii. Price

    iv. Placement

  c. Marketing Tactics

III. **Evaluation and Control**

  a. Determine what to measure.

  b. Set performance standards.

  c. Measure actual performance.

  d. Compare actual performance with standards.

  e. Determine the reasons for discrepancies.

  f. Take corrective action.

Table 10.1   Components of the Implementation Marketing Plan

■ Are channels in place to allow the client to openly communicate the features and characteristics it is looking for in the IS?

- Does the client have a realistic sense of what it can and what it cannot demand of the project team?
- Are there any reasons to believe that the client would not readily perceive or act to correct problem areas that could eventually lead to the client's rejection of the new system?

- Client's tolerance range regarding cost, time, and performance criteria
    - What are the client's expectations concerning total project costs?
    - Does the client have a realistic sense of when the project will be completed?
    - Has the client made its expectations known regarding such system-performance criteria as quality, reliability, safety, function, capabilities, and so on?
    - What criteria are being used by the client to evaluate the acceptability of the product of the project?
    - Client's ability to accept transference of the completed product
    - Does the client have the technical knowledge required to make use of the completed product?
    - Does the anticipated project completion date coincide with the date the client will be ready for the system?
    - Are backup systems or resources in place in the client's organization that will facilitate the implementation of the IS?
    - Does the client have a realistic sense of what it must do to prepare for the effective transfer and implementation of the system?

- Political support within the client's organization
    - Are existing or future projects in the client's organization in any way jeopardized by the new project?
    - Do influential persons in the client's organization support the project?
    - What changes will be required by the project that may be perceived as threatening by those in the client's organization who can affect the success of the IS?
    - What do specific members or groups in the client's organization have to lose or gain if the system is successfully implemented?

These questions are presented as examples of the types of questions that could be relevant to each issue area, and they may not necessarily provide the information essential for an adequate client analysis in all instances. In order to ensure reasonable comprehensiveness in client analyses, project team members are urged to continually consider why the client analysis is being performed.

First, the analysis can furnish the team with the information needed to ensure that its system will serve the client more efficiently and effectively than other products or alternatives. Second, such an analysis will enable team members to learn the pros and cons of the project from the client's point of view. Both of these concerns will have a major impact on the marketability of the project. With these thoughts in mind, project team members can formulate a tailored list of questions designed to provide information relating to the attractiveness of their projects.

INFORMATION SYSTEM MARKETING STRATEGY

Information gathered in the client analysis is used as the basis for formulating the IS implementation *sales* strategy. The key question here is which marketing-related objectives and tactics should the implementation team choose in order to best ensure that the prospective users will be sold on the new system.

Setting the marketing objectives. In establishing marketing objectives for the implementation effort, it is useful to think in terms of the four P's of marketing: price, product, place, and promotion (Bagozzi 1987). The information gathered in the client analysis will suggest what should be the appropriate marketing objective in each of these areas. For example, one of the aforementioned system-marketing issue areas is the client's tolerance range with regard to critical project cost, timing, and performance criteria. If the implementation team knows what budget for system acquisition, installation, and subsequent personnel training costs the client is willing to accept in the IS, the team can develop an acceptable system-price objective from the client's point of view. Information gathered in another of the previously mentioned system-marketing areas, the client's needs, could suggest what attributes the system should possess. Accordingly, a client-needs assessment will often provide information that is helpful in establishing optimal *product* objectives.

Place objectives may be inferable from information gathered on the client's ability to accept transference of the acquired system. Establishing particular competence levels among one's clients in the proper use of a technologically sophisticated product such as an IS, for example, is a place objective that relates to how readily the client will accept the new system.

Finally, knowledge of the level of support within the organization can suggest the need to establish particular *promotion* objectives. To illustrate, objectives could be set regarding the need to educate certain individuals or groups about the advantages that would accrue to the client departments if they adopted and used the IS technology. In short, information relating to each of the implementation-marketing issue areas can be used as a basis for setting the marketing objectives for the acquired IS.

Choosing the marketing tactics. Marketing tactics are the specific means chosen to achieve the objectives relating to price, product, place, and promotion. These tactics must collectively allow the implementation team to fulfill the wants and needs of the client, if they are to be judged successful. As noted by Culliton (1986, 4), "The key to successful marketing lies in having the right product at the right price at the right place (time) with the right promotion and ... the rightness of the elements is determined by the customer." The same principle applies to marketing a newly acquired system, such as an IS.

The appropriate tactics for achieving particular IS marketing objectives will often be fairly obvious to the team and IS manager. For example, strict adherence to budget targets in acquiring, installing, and training personnel would be a logical means for achieving rigorous implementation cost objectives.

Sometimes, however, the identification of appropriate marketing tactics will not be an easy task. Fortunately, just as the client analysis will suggest the establishment of particular marketing objectives, it can provide information on the marketing tactics through which those objectives should be sought. For example, suppose that an IS marketing objective in the promotion area is to ensure that the functional performance capabilities of the acquired IS are fully understood by the departments targeted to make use of the system. Let us assume that two competing promotion tactics are being considered in order to attain this objective: 1) personal discussions with all members of the client departments, whose jobs will in some way be influenced by the project, or, 2) the provision of technical literature to those departments' contact people or representatives. An analysis of the political support within the organization for the system could suggest that the latter promotional tactic would be an ineffective way to achieve the stated objective.

Team involvement. As a final thought, we should note that one's choice of implementation-marketing strategy and tactics is too critical to be automatically decided by a single implementation team member, including the leader of the effort. An acceptable marketing strategy-decision process will typically require the input of multiple members of the project team, especially if the team is composed of members from different functional departments or with various degrees of experience and background. The key here is diversity. Certainly, technical questions must be addressed by those technically capable of dealing with these problems. Remember, however, that a variety of other issues—many of them political or behavioral—are often the catalyst for successful IS adoption. The manager who selects a homogenous team will miss a great deal of powerful brainstorming from individuals who see things from different perspectives. Group or participative decision-making from a set of diverse team members will maximize the probability that marketing-strategy decisions are based on the best information of the project team. Such a decision process also conveys the important symbolic message that system-marketing strategy is too important to be based on anything but the implementation team's most thorough understanding of the clients.

EVALUATION AND CONTROL

The final phase of an IS-implementation marketing plan is composed of evaluation and control activities. The purpose of this phase is to ensure that the system is being marketed to the clients in the manner specified by the IS marketing strategy (Pride and Ferrell 1987). The evaluation and control process consists of six steps.

1. Determine what to measure: The marketing-related criteria used to set the objectives determine what should be measured. These measures could include issues such as level of client familiarity with the performance characteristics (the system as a product), client expectations regarding the implementation team's assistance in transferring the system to the clients, and client sensitivity regarding possible adjustments in the cost of the installed IS technology.

2. Set performance standards: *Performance standard* is simply another way of saying *marketing objective*—that is, the marketing objectives established in the preceding phase of the marketing plan represent the performance standards.

3. Measure actual performance: This step involves an honest assessment of the implementation team's achieved results in terms of marketing the system. It is more than establishing a scheduling measurement and control system like those mentioned in Chapter 5, such as PERT/CPM and Gantt charts. Rather, it is the determination, in as fair a manner as possible, of whether or not the implementation is meeting its goals in terms of selling the acquired IS to the client departments. For example, the number of telephone calls from the accounting department office asking for help in system crashes and debugging problems, or time spent answering questions regarding performance characteristics, could be some of the criteria used to assess how well the IS was marketed.

4. Compare actual performance with performance standards: How does the achieved level of performance stack up against the objectives established in these areas? A minimal gap between the two would suggest that the IS marketing objectives are being achieved. A significant or prolonged gap between standards and actual performance would indicate

that the implementation team is not doing its job in marketing the system to the clients.

5. Determine the reason for any observed discrepancy: There are any number of reasons why the IS marketing strategy is not producing the intended results. The client analysis upon which the marketing strategy is based may have been unrealistic; the system marketing tactics chosen to achieve these objectives may have been inappropriate for the task or poorly executed. In any case, it is vital that the IS implementation team determine why the marketing strategy is not producing the desired results.

6. Take corrective action: Once the reasons for observed problems have been identified, the project team needs to take the necessary steps to correct the problem. Whether that action involves reshaping its presentation to the client departments, collecting more information, or engaging in additional selling activities, steps must be taken to bring the marketing strategy back into effective operation.

Collectively, the three phases of the IS marketing plan—1) client analysis, 2) formulating marketing strategy and tactics, and, 3) engaging in implementation marketing control and evaluation—constitute a simple but effective process for increasing the likelihood of client acceptance of the proposed IS. Each of these phases is distinct but ties together well when put into actual practice. In short, the IS-implementation marketing plan can be a very helpful and powerful tool for IS managers concerned with the downstream results of their efforts.

Managerial Implications

Several specific managerial implications follow from the discussion of the marketing process for IS innovations.

New systems, whether IS or any other form, are not intended to be developed in a vacuum. Effective system implementation must be developed from its earliest conceptual phase with regard to customers. In many instances, particularly within R&D settings or pure IS research, we are so caught up in the actual development process that we ignore the bottom-line determinant of success: Can we sell the system; in other words, will it be used? Managers charged with implementing IS in their organizations need to engage in active communication with potential and/or solidified clients from the earliest stages to determine their specific needs and concerns. The point is to fit the IS to your department, rather than attempting to alter departmental attitudes to accommodate the IS that has already been acquired.

Successful IS implementation means successful system introduction. As Chapter 3, on implementation success, goes to great length to demonstrate, technical validity (does the system work?) is only part of the determinant of success. No IS will ever be considered successfully adopted if it is not used. Simply exhibiting concern for the technical merits of an IS is inconsistent with the current realities of system installation and management in most modern workplaces. Getting the system up and running on time, within budget, and in accordance with its advertised performance specifications is useless unless it is being used. Further, that use must lead to some form of enhanced decision-making or other measure of greater organizational effectiveness. Anything short of this set of success criteria simply misses the mark.

Even while planning the implementation, plan for its marketing strategy. Although most project life cycles often point to some form of termination stage, when the system is turned over to the clients, it is important to note that truly effective project managers begin planning for the transition to the client long before the system enters its final phase (Spirer and Hamburger 1988). The implementation-marketing plan this chapter offers represents a framework from which the IS manager and team can begin, at an early stage, developing a plan for selling the completed product to its clients. This plan would be subject to further refinement throughout the system-implementation process. As changes are made to the system, or as capabilities are altered, changes to the marketing plan would also be required. As a result, by the time the implementation team has begun to wind the project down, it will have maintained an updated strategy for successfully marketing the final product to its intended users.

Conclusions

This chapter offers some suggestions for considering an aspect of implementation that has long been ignored, but that can have a tremendous impact on the success or failure of IS implementation: project marketing. While some managers may have long attended to this function, a majority of IS managers, even if interested, have not had a systematic method by which they can do an effective job of ensuring client acceptance. The framework this chapter offers is for helping implementation teams address issues of client acceptance through developing an implementation marketing plan. Many project managers, in a variety of settings, have found that project teams that devote sufficient time to selling their projects often reap substantial dividends. It is hoped that through use of this framework other IS managers who are new to the process and the necessity of selling their systems will be in a better position to ensure client acceptance and, consequently, greater IS implementation success.

11

Conclusions: Quo Vadis?

> People are generally persuaded better by the reasons which they themselves have discovered than by those which have come into the mind of others.
>
> *Blaise Pascal*

The Latin term, *quo vadis*, asks us where we are going. In other words, where do we go from here? What conclusions can be reached about the process of information systems (IS) implementation? Certainly it should be quite apparent that IS implementation is characterized by enormous difficulty, ambiguity, and personal challenge. It is in answering this personal challenge that IS managers run into a battery of impediments to adoption success, including organizational politics, user apathy, lukewarm and changeable support from top management, and so forth. Coupled with the current lack of practical guideposts and supporting management literature, it is little wonder that implementing IS is such a challenging and often frustrating activity.

This book seeks to squarely address the issue of IS implementation, specifically arguing that the implementation challenge is a human challenge; that is, its success or failure is based on a wide variety of behavioral and organizational issues that the IS project manager must address. Books focusing solely on the technology of IS have been and continue to be an important part of the literature. Unfortunately, as our understanding of the technical side of information has continued to expand, our ability to effectively manage these systems has not kept pace. The overwhelmingly technical emphasis that exists in the IS literature is a natural response to a technology that is just beginning to take off. As more and better applications and user-friendly features are developed for the systems, it is time to begin rounding out those areas that have experienced neglect, and one obvious area is that of implementing and managing IS.

We suspect that part of the reason that implementation issues have been left unresolved for so long lies in the relative *newness* of information technology. The exciting aspect of these systems lies in our ability and eagerness to constantly upgrade and refine the technology. Tacitly, there seems to be a general assumption that once the technical bugs are worked out of IS, the systems will simply sell themselves. This narrow mindedness is exemplified by a recent conversation one of the authors had with an IS engineer, who was genuinely mystified by statements concerning the need to manage the implementation of IS. His statement—"The systems work. Of course companies will use them!"—reflects the longstanding but misguided notion of a number of individuals who assume that important new technologies are:

- readily apparent to all
- eagerly awaited by all.

Our research, consulting, and organizational experience suggests just the opposite; in fact, it roundly rejects the notion that any form of organizational change, such as that offered by adopting IS technology, is in for a smooth transition to organizational acceptance and use. People do feel threatened by change. They grow comfortable with inertia, even when it means more work or less efficient operations.

It is in consequence of this gap in the IS literature that this book has been written. Implementing IS, or any other advanced technology, is a challenge and requires a strategy and methodology all its own. We have offered a wide range of issues devoted to both the context of implementation, as well as some of the more important acts and actors in the implementation process. It is hoped that readers will find something of themselves, as well as something of use, contained in these pages.

Points to Keep in Mind

We have gone back through the topics presented in this book to glean out some of the more salient issues that need to be kept in mind when initiating a system introduction. Although not intended to appear in any particular order, this set of ten rules offers a convenient way to synthesize much of the material that was developed in more detail throughout the book.

---

1. Lead flexibly.

2. Understand what implementation success means.

3. The client is number one.

4. Learn and use the political system to your advantage.

5. Find a champion.

6. Build and maintain a cohesive team.

7. Enthusiasm and despair are both infectious.

8. One look forward is worth two looks back.

9. Remember what you are trying to do.

10. Plan to succeed, or you plan to fail.

Table 11.1   Points to Remember

---

1. Lead flexibly: The essence of leadership lies in our ability to use it flexibly. Some situations and subordinate relationships will require very autocratic approaches, while others will be far better served by a consensual style. Effective leaders understand this idea intuitively. Their approach must be tailored to the situation; it is self-defeating to attempt to tailor the situation to a preferred approach. The worst *leaders* are those who are unaware of or indifferent to the freedom they have to vary their leadership styles. This point was recently reinforced with one of the authors when a mid-level manager asserted, "I'm eminently fair. I treat all my subordinates the same." The better-informed readers can immediately see the obvious contradiction. Subordinates are not the same. Why, then, do we make the mistake of treating them as if they were? Until managers learn to vary their leadership styles, to include a wide medley of situational criteria, they will never begin to realize the potential they possess as team leaders.

2. Understand what implementation *success* means: Successful implementation is not simply getting the system installed on time and within budget; in fact, in many ways, that is the easy part. The difficulty lies in fulfilling the other success criteria, including gaining client acceptance and use and, further, creating a system that is perceived to improve organizational effectiveness. This suggests that success is a far more comprehensive word than some managers may have initially thought. The implication for rewards is also important. Within some organizations, it is common practice to reward the implementation manager when in reality

only half the job has been accomplished. In other words, giving managers promotions and commendations before the system is being used and is impacting on organization effectiveness is seriously jumping the gun.

3. The client is number one: This point emanates from the one above. An implemented system is only as good as it is used. In the final analysis, nothing else matters if a system is not productively employed. Consequently, every effort must be bent toward ensuring that the system fits clients' needs, that clients' concerns and opinions are solicited and heard, and that clients have final sign-off approval on the IS installation. The intended user of the IS is the major determinant of its success. As the reader can tell, we are passionate on this point—because we have seen in far too many situations mere lip service paid to the needs of the intended user. The bulk of the team's efforts are centered internally, mainly on its own concerns: budgets, timetables, and so forth. Certainly, these aspects of the implementation process are necessary, but they should not be confused with the ultimate determinant of success: the client.

4. Learn and use the political system to your advantage: Like it or not, we exist in a politicized world. Unfortunately, our organizations are no different. Important decisions are made through bargaining and deal making. IS managers wishing to succeed must learn to use the political system to their advantage. This use involves negotiation and using influence tactics to further the goals of the implementation effort. Remember that any organizational change is threatening, often due to its potential to reshuffle the power relationships among the key organizational units and actors. Playing the political system simply acknowledges this reality, and argues that successful IS managers are those who can use their personal power and influence to smooth the adoption of the system.

5. Find a champion: Champions are an important element in system acquisition and adoption. Their single-mindedness and enthusiasm are tremendous sources of energy for the implementation team. Further, they serve to publicize the system and keep it in the forefront of top management's mind. While they may occasionally act as organizational gadflies, their benefits far outweigh their drawbacks. If a champion for the IS does exist, support that individual. She can do a lot for the adoption of a new system, but she needs her own backers. In sum, my advice is to listen to champions, support them, and put them to work.

6. Build and maintain a cohesive team: When a team is tasked to work toward IS adoption, the healthier the atmosphere within that team, the greater the likelihood that the team will perform effectively. The manager's job is to do whatever is necessary to build and maintain the health (cohesion) of the implementation team. Sometimes that support can be accomplished by periodically checking with team members to determine their attitudes and satisfaction with the process. Other times, the manager

may have to resort to less conventional methods, such as throwing parties or organizing group field trips for the team. In order to effectively intervene and support a team, managers play a variety of roles including motivator, cheer leader, peace maker, and conflict resolver. All of these duties are appropriate in creating and maintaining an effective team.

7. Enthusiasm and despair are both infectious: Implementation team leaders often function like miniaturized billboards. They project an image and attitude that signals the current status of the system and its likelihood for success. The team takes its cue from the attitudes and emotions that the manager exhibits. As leader, one of the most important roles is that of motivator and encourager. The worst type of team managers are those who play their cards close to their chests, revealing little or nothing about the status of the project. Team members want and need to be kept abreast of what is happening. Remember, the success or failure of the IS implementation affects the team, as well as the manager. Rather than allowing the rumor mill to churn out disinformation, team leaders need to function as honest sources of information. When team members come to you for advice or project updates, be honest. If you do not know the answer to their questions, tell them you do not know. Truth in all forms is recognizable, and most team members are much more appreciative of honesty than eyewash.

8. One look forward is worth two looks back: A recent series of commercials from a large computer manufacturer had as its slogan the dictum that it never stops asking, "What if?" Asking the what-if questions is another way of saying that we should never become comfortable about the status of the implementation. As we mentioned in Chapter 4, on critical success factors, the number-one determinant of project success is the absence of any troubleshooting mechanisms—that is, anyone asking the what-if questions. Projecting a skeptical eye toward the future may seem gloomy to some managers; in my opinion, it makes good sense. We cannot control the future, but, if we are proactive, we can control our response to it.

9. Remember what you are trying to do: Do not lose sight of the purpose behind the IS installation. Sometimes it is easy to get bogged down in the minutia of the process and fail to maintain a view of what the end product is supposed to be. This point reemphasizes the need to keep the mission in the forefront, not just for the manager but for the team as well. The goal of the implementation serves as a large banner that the team leader can wave as needed to keep attitudes and motives focused in the right direction. Sometimes a superordinate goal can serve as this rallying point. Whatever technique project managers use, it is important that they understand the importance of keeping the mission in focus for all team members. A simple technique for assessing team members'

understanding of the project is to intermittently ask for their assessment of the project's status. Further, they should be aware of how their contributions fit into the overall installation plan. Are they aware of the specific contributions of other team members? If the answer is no, more attention needs to be paid to reestablishing a community sense of mission.

Remember that change orders and their accompanying *scope creep* are project killers. Far too many projects run into huge budget and schedule overruns because either the project manager or top management allowed the project to grow and change in midstream. Obviously, in the case of technical problems, it is appropriate to consider change orders. The flaw becomes apparent, however, when we consider that the majority of change requests are to add new features (*bells and whistles*) to the system as it undergoes development. Each bell and whistle adds to system cost, project rework cycles, and schedule delays. The better project managers are at keeping their projects under control and avoiding excessive scope creep, the greater the odds of bringing the project in successfully.

10. Plan to succeed, or you plan to fail. Many of us are aware of the adage that those who fail to plan are planning to fail. There is a great deal of truth in this statement. Planning is a necessary, albeit often unglamorous, aspect of the implementation process. Planning can be particularly onerous when top management begins agitating for prompt action from the team. The best weapon that project managers have to deal with impatient upper management is communication: Keep members of upper management informed. Remember: "If they know nothing of what you are doing, they assume you are doing nothing." This point is particularly relevant during the planning stage because, as far as upper management can tell, nothing is happening. In that situation, the leader of the implementation may start receiving increasingly anxious memos from top management, wondering when activity on the IS installation will commence. What these individuals do not realize is that activity may have already commenced, in the form of project planning. Planning is an important condition of success, and its status must be communicated to top management, the clients, and other organizational stakeholders.

These ten points are intended to put into simpler terms some of the most important elements in the IS implementation process. Much more can be said about each of these topics, and within the various chapters of this book they are developed to a considerable degree. It was our purpose in writing this book to begin to uncover and make plain some of the most important issues in implementation, whether used in implementing IS, other systems, or, indeed, any form of organizational innovation. When addressed from the behavioral and organizational perspectives, we can begin to attend to the implementation process in both an effective and efficient manner. One of the reasons why so little has been written to date in the area of IS implementation is that the technology is still, in many ways, in its infancy. Although the *novelty* aspect of IS has long ago worn off, as more and more public and private organizations acquire the technology, many argue that we are still in the early adoption phase of its diffusion. Consequently, the lion's share of writing and practice has been directed toward pure research and applications-oriented issues.

Directions for the Future

The first edition of *Successful Information System Implementation* represented one of the few early efforts aimed at the development of insights and considerations for IS implementation. Although there is a wealth of case studies and anecdotal material on the implementation problem, there are few formal, empirical studies upon which to base a theoretical foundation for adopting IS. While this dearth of theory-based research is unfortunate, in another sense it represents both a challenge and a great opportunity for IS researchers. IS implementation research as a discipline is uniquely positioned to be addressed by researchers from organizational, behavioral, and even technical perspectives. Part of this opportunity is due to timing. We suggest that IS technology has long passed from its infancy to a stage of expansion and growth. Although the technology is well known, the problems with implementing and gaining organizational acceptance for these systems only continue to grow. Consequently, there is currently a true window of opportunity in the field of IS adoption.

Although it is not our objective to develop a metric by which future implementation research should be judged, there are some points that need to be considered if future adoption theory and practice are to be relevant to the great majority of managers in organizations using IS. First, the research should be predicated on grounded and existing theory. An enormous quantity of research exists—exploring issues in new system implementation, diffusion of innovations, project management, and so forth—that is very relevant to continuing work in IS project management. There are important issues in data collection, construct measurement, and statistical procedures that can be employed in our work in IS, saving researchers from having to reinvent wheels, and instead allowing us to learn from other scientists' mistakes.

Another point that bears consideration is the need to apply accepted research techniques to our studies. The well-developed field of research in social science is one that offers the IS researcher an excellent starting point for theory construction and research-technique development. We need to apply these systematic and thorough research approaches to our efforts, if we are to offer truly generalizable findings that have the potential to influence IS theory and management practice. Finally, although there are areas of commonality with other previously developed disciplines (such as operations management), we need to explore in detail the issues that make IS theory and research distinct. What is it about IS technology and implementation issues that is unique and can be communicated to managers? While these questions are easily answered from a technical perspective, they are at once more subtle, more profound, and indeed key in addressing the behavioral and managerial questions surrounding the use of IS technology.

It is our continued hope that this book does not simply become the last word in IS implementation, but rather sparks an increased awareness and interest in the field. Although IS technology is exciting, because it is still evolving and new, issues of IS management are even more embryonic. If, as a result of reading this book, others in both the academic and practitioner communities are energized and motivated to devote attention to the topic, the field of implementation research will be well served, and we will be well rewarded.

References

Allen, R. W., D. L. Madison, L. W. Porter, P. A. Renwick, and B. Y. Moyes. 1979. Organizational Politics: Tactics and Characteristics of Actors. *California Management Review* 22 (1): 78.

Antenucci, J. C., K. Brown, P. L. Croswell, and M. Kevany. 1991. *Geographic Information Systems: A Guide to the Technology.* New York: Van Nostrand Reinhold.

Arnoff, E. L. 1971. *Successful Models I Have Known.* Decision Sciences, vol. 2, 141–48.

Bagozzi, R. P. 1987. *Principles of Marketing Management.* Chicago, IL: Science Research Associates.

Baker, B. N., D. C. Murphy, and D. Fisher. 1988. Factors Affecting Project Success. In *Project Management Handbook,* edited by D. I. Cleland and W. R. King. New York: Van Nostrand Reinhold, 902–19

Bean, A. S., and M. Radnor. 1979. The Role of Intermediaries in the Implementation of Management Science. In R. Doktor, R. L. Schultz, and D. P. Slevin (Eds.), *The Implementation of Management Science,* New York: North-Holland, 121–38.

Beck, D. R. 1983. Implementing Top Management Plans Through Project Management. In *Project Management Handbook,* edited by D. I. Cleland and W. R. King. New York: Van Nostrand Reinhold, 166–84.

Beeman, D. R., and T. W. Sharkey. 1987. The Use and Abuse of Corporate Politics. *Business Horizons* 36 (2): 26–30.

Blake, R. R., and J. Mouton. 1964. *The Managerial Grid.* Houston, TX: Gulf Publishing.

Blanchard, K. H., and P. Zigarmi. 1985. *Leadership and the One-Minute Manager.* New York: Morrow.

Bower, M., and R. A. Garda. 1986. The Role of Marketing in Management. In *The Handbook of Modern Marketing,* 2d ed. New York: McGraw-Hill, 3–15.

Chakrabarti, A. K. 1974. The Role of Champion in Product Innovation. *California Management Review* 17 (2): 58–62.

Churchman, C. W., and H. A. Schainblatt. 1965. The Researcher and the Manager: A Dialectic of Implementation. *Management Science* 11: 1369–87.

CIO. 1995 (Nov. 15), 5.

Covin, J. G., and D. P. Slevin. 1988. The Influence of Organization Structure on the Utility of an Entrepreneurial Top Management Style. *Journal of Management Studies* 25: 217–34.

Croswell, P. L. 1989. Facing Reality in GIS Implementation: Lessons Learned and Obstacles to Be Overcome. *Proceedings of the Urban and Regional Information Systems Association.* Boston, MA: Washington D.C.: Urban & Regional Information Systems Association. Vol. 4: pp. 15–35. (Reprinted in *Journal of the Urban and Regional Information Systems Association* 3, no. 1 (1991): 43–56).

Culliton, J. W. 1986. The Concept of the Marketing Mix. In *The Handbook of Modern Marketing*, 2d ed. New York: McGraw-Hill, 3–13.

Dansereau, F., G. Graen, and B. Haga. 1975. A Vertical Dyad Linkage Approach to Leadership within Formal Organizations: A Longitudinal Investigation of Role Making Process. *Organizational Behavior and Human Performance* 13: 45–78.

Davis, T. E. 1984. The Influence of the Physical Environment in Offices. *Academy of Management Review* 9 (2): 271–83.

DeLone, W. H., and E. R. McLean. 1992. Information Systems Success: The Quest for the Dependent Variable. *Information Systems Research* 3: 60–95.

Ein-Dor, Phillip, Eli Segev, Doron Blumenthal, and Ido Millet. 1984. Perceived Importance, Investment and Success of MIS, or the MIS Zoo—An Empirical Investigation and a Taxonomy. *Systems, Objectives, Solutions* 4, no. 2: 61–67.

Einsiedel, A. A. 1987. Profile of Effective Project Managers. *Project Management Journal* 18 (5): 51–56.

Fiedler, F. E. 1978. Contingency Models and the Leadership Process. In *Advances in Experimental Social Psychology*, vol. 11, edited by L. Berkowitz. New York: Academic Press.

Fleishman, E. A. 1973. Twenty Years of Consideration and Structure. In *Current Developments in the Study of Leadership*, edited by E. A. Fleishman and J. G. Hunt. Carbondale, IL: Southern Illinois UP.

Fodor, E. M. 1976. Group Stress, Authoritarian Style of Control, and Use of Power. *Journal of Applied Psychology* 61: 313–18.

Fortune. 1989. The U.S. Must Do as GM Has Done. February: 70–79.

Freedman, Daniel P., and Gerald M. Weinberg. 1990. *Handbook of Walkthroughs, Inspections, and Technical Reviews.* New York: Dorset House.

French, J. R. P., and B. Raven. 1959. The Bases of Social Power. In *Studies in Social Power*, edited by D. Cartwright. Ann Arbor, MI: Institute for Social Research, 150–67.

Galbraith, J. R. 1977. *Organization Design.* Reading, MA: Addison-Wesley.

Gandz, J., and V. V. Murray. 1980. Experiences of Workplace Politics. *Academy of Management Journal* 23: 237–51.

Ghiselli, E. 1971. *Exploration of Managerial Talent.* Santa Monica, CA: Goodyear.

Ginzberg, M. J. 1978. Finding an Adequate Measure of OR/MS Effectiveness. *Interfaces* 8, no. 4, 59–62.

Graham, R. J. 1992. Private communication.

Gronn, P. 1993. Psychobiography on the Couch: Character, Biography, and the Comparative Study of Leaders. *Journal of Applied Behavioral Science* 29: 343–58.

Hammond, J. S., III. 1979. A Practitioner-Oriented Framework for Implementation. In *The Implementation of Management Science*, edited by R. Doktor, R. L. Schultz, and D. P. Slevin. New York: North-Holland, 35–62

Heilman, M. E., H. A. Hornstein, J. H. Cage, and J. K. Herschlag. 1984. Reactions to a Prescribed Leader Behavior as a Function of Role Perspective: The Case of the Vroom-Yetton Model. *Journal of Applied Psychology* 69: 50–60.

Hickson, D. J., C. R. Hinings, C. A. Lee, R. E. Schneck, and J. M. Pennings. 1971. A Strategic Contingencies Theory of Intraorganizational Power. *Administrative Sciences Quarterly* 16: 216–29.

House, R. J. 1971. A Path-Goal Theory of Leadership Effectiveness. *Administrative Science Quarterly* 16: 321–33.

Huxhold, W. E. 1991. *An Introduction to Urban Geographic Information Systems.* New York: Oxford University Press.

Infoworld. 1995 (Feb. 6), 62.

Javidan, M., and A. Dastmachian. 1993. Assessing Senior Executives: The Impact of Context on Their Roles. *Journal of Applied Behavioral Science* 29: 328–42.

Kapur, G. K. 1998. Don't Look Back to Create the Future. Address given at the Frontiers of Project Management conference, Boston, MA (May).

Keen, P. G. W. 1980. Reference Disciplines and a Cumulative Tradition. *Proceedings of the First International Conference on Information Systems*, 9–18.

Kerr, S., and J. M. Jermier. 1978. Substitutes for Leadership: Their Meaning and Measurement. *Organizational Behavior and Human Performance* 22: 375–403.

Kolb, D. A., and A. L. Frohman. 1970. An Organizational Development Approach to Consulting. *Sloan Management Review* 12: 51–65.

Kotler, P. 1980. *Marketing Management: Analysis, Planning, and Control*, 4th ed. Englewood Cliffs, NJ: Prentice-Hall.

Kouzes, J. M., and B. Z. Posner. 1991. *The Leadership Challenge.* San Francisco, CA: Jossey-Bass.

Lawrence, P. R., and J. W. Lorsch. 1967. Differentiation and Integration in Complex Organizations. *Adminstrative Science Quarterly* 11: 1–47.

———. 1969. *Organization and Environment.* Homewood, IL: Irwin.

Leana, C. R. 1986. Predictors and Consequences of Delegation. *Academy of Management Journal* 29: 754–74.

Leibson, D. E. 1981. How Corning Designed a "Talking" Building to Spur Productivity. *Management Review* 70: 8–13.

Levinsohn, A. G. 1989. A Strategic Planning Based Approach to the Design of Land Information Systems. *Proceedings of the Urban and Regional Information System Association*, vol. 2: 30–38. Washington, DC: Urban and Regional Information Systems Association.

Lewin, K., and E. Schein. 1952. Group Decision and Social Change. In *Readings in Social Psychology*, edited by Newcomb and Hartley. New York: Holt, 459–75.

Lucas, H. J., Jr. 1975. Behavioral Factors in System Implementation. In *Implementing Operations Research and Management Science*, edited by R. L. Schultz and D. P. Slevin. New York: Elsevier, 203–16.

Maidique, M. A. 1980. Entrepreneurs, Champions, and Technological Innovation. *Sloan Management Review* 21 (Winter): 59–76.

Manley, J. H. 1975. Implementation Attitudes: A Model and a Measurement Methodology. In *Implementing Operations Research/Management Science*, edited by R. L. Schultz and D. P. Slevin. New York: Elsevier, 183–202.

March, J. G., and H. A. Simon. 1958. *Organizations*. New York: John Wiley.

Markus, M. L. 1983. Power, Politics, and MIS Implementation. *Communications of the ACM* 19: 321–42.

Mayes, B. T., and R. W. Allen. 1977. Toward a Definition of Organizational Politics. *Academy of Management Review* 2: 675.

Meredith, J. A. 1986. Strategic Planning for Factory Automation by the Championing Process. *IEEE Transactions on Engineering Management* EM-33 (4): 229–32.

Millet, Ido. 1994. Who's on First? *CIO* (Feb. 15).

Mintzberg, H. 1983. *Power In and Around Organizations*. Englewood Cliffs, NJ: Prentice Hall.

Mitroff, I. I. 1975. On Mutual Understanding and the Implementation Problem: A Philosophical Case Study of the Psychology of the Apollo Moon Scientists. In *Implementing Operations Research and Management Science*, edited by R.L. Schultz and D.P. Slevin. New York: Elsevier, 237–52.

Morris, P. W. G. 1983. Managing Project Interfaces: Key Points for Project Success. In *Project Management Handbook*, edited by D. I. Cleland and W. R. King. New York: Van Nostrand Reinhold, 3–36.

Onsrud, H. J., H. W. Calkins, and N. J. Obermeyer, eds. 1989. Use and Value of Geographic Information: Initiative Four Specialist Meeting Report and Proceedings, National Center for Geographic Information and Analysis, Technical Paper 89-7, University of California, Santa Barbara.

Onsrud, H. J., and J. K. Pinto. 1993. Evaluating Correlates of GIS Adoption Success and the Decision Process of GIS Acquisition. *Journal of the Urban and Regional Information Systems Association* 5: 18–39.

Paulk, Mark C., Bill Curtis, Mary Beth Chrissis, and Charles V. Weber. 1993. Capability Maturity Model for Software, Version 1.1. Software Engineering Institute CMU/SEI-93-TR-24, DTIC Number ADA263403 (Feb.).

Paulk, Mark C., Charles V. Weber, Suzanne M. Garcia, Mary Beth Chrissis, and Marilyn W. Bush. 1993. Key Practices of the Capability Maturity Model, Version 1.1. Software Engineering Institute CMU/SEI-93-TR-25, CTIC Number ADA263432 (Feb.).

Peters, M. P. 1986. Innovation for Hospitals: An Application of the Product Development Process. *Journal of Health Care Marketing* 29: 182–91.

Peters, T. A. 1985. A Passion for Excellence. *Fortune* (May 13).

Pettersen, N. 1991. What Do We Know about the Effective Project Manager? *International Journal of Project Management* 9: 99–104.

Pfeffer, J. 1981. *Power in Organizations*. Marshfield, MA: Pitman.

Pinto, J. K., and S. J. Mantel Jr. 1990. The Causes of Project Failure. *IEEE Transactions on Engineering Management* EM-37: 269–76.

Pinto, J. K., and D. P. Slevin. 1987. Critical Factors in Successful Project Implementation. *IEEE Transactions on Engineering Management* EM-34: 1, 22–27.

———. 1988a. Critical Success Factors Across the Project Life Cycle. *Project Management Journal* 19 (3): 67–75.

———. 1988b. The Project Champion: Key to Implementation Success. *Project Management Journal* 20 (4): 15–20.

Pinto, J. K., P. Thoms, J. Trailer, T. Palmer, and M. Govekar. 1998. *Project Leadership: From Theory to Practice.* Newtown Square, PA: Project Management Institute.

Pinto, M. B. 1988. Cross-Functional Cooperation in the Implementation of Marketing Decisions: The Effects of Superordinate Goals, Rules and Procedures, and Physical Environment. Unpublished Doctoral Dissertation, University of Pittsburgh, PA.

PMI Standards Committee. *A Guide to the Project Management Body of Knowledge.* Upper Darby, PA: Project Management Institute.

Posner, B. Z. 1987. What It Takes to Be a Good Project Manager. *Project Management Journal* 18 (1): 51–54.

Pregent, T. 1988. Private communication.

Pride, W. M., and O. C. Ferrell. 1987. *Marketing: Basic Concepts and Decisions.* Boston, MA: Houghton-Mifflin Co.

Rice, R. E., and E. M. Rogers. 1980. *Re-Invention in the Innovation Process. Knowledge: Creation, Implementation, Utilization.* Vol. 1, 499–514.

Rogers, E. M. 1983. *Implementation of Innovations,* 3d ed. New York: The Free Press.

Salancik, G. R., B. J. Calder, K. M. Rowland, H. Leblibici, and M. Conway. 1975. Leadership as an Outcome of Social Structure and Process: A Multi-Dimensional Analysis. In *Leadership Frontiers,* edited by J. G. Hunt and L. L. Larson. Kent, OH: Kent State UP.

Schon, D. A. 1967. *Technology and Change.* New York: Delacorte.

Schultz, R. L. and M. D. Henry. 1981. Implementing Decision Models. In *Marketing Decision Models,* edited by R.L. Schultz and A.A. Zoltners. New York: North-Holland, 123–34.

Schultz, R. L., and D. P. Slevin. 1975a. Implementation and Management Innovation. In *Implementing Operations Research/Management Science,* edited by R. L. Schultz and D. P. Slevin. New York: Elsevier, 3–20.

———. 1975b. Implementation and Organizational Validity: An Empirical Investigation. In *Implementing Operations Research/Management Science,* edited by R. L. Schultz and D. P. Slevin. New York: Elsevier, 153–82.

———. 1979. Introduction: The Implementation Problem. In *The Implementation of Management Science,* edited by R. Doktor, R. L. Schultz, and D. P. Slevin. New York: North-Holland, 1–15.

Schultz, R. L., D. P. Slevin, and J. K. Pinto. 1987. Strategy and Tactics in a Process Model of Project Implementation. *Interfaces* 17 (3): 34–46.

Schultz, R. L., M. J. Ginzberg, and H. C. Lucas Jr. 1983. A Structural Model of Implementation. University of Texas Working Paper.

Schweiger, David M., William R. Sandberg, and Paula L. Rechner. 1989. Experiential Effects of Dialectical Inquiry, Devil's Advocacy, and Consensus Approaches to Strategic Decision-Making. *Academy of Management Journal* 32 (4): 745–72.

Schwenk, Charles. 1990a. Effects of Devil's Advocacy and Dialectical Inquiry on Decision-Making: A Meta-Analysis. *Organizational Behavior and Human Decision Processes* 36: 161–76.

———. 1990b. Conflict in Organizational Decision-Making: An Exploratory Study of Its Effects in For-Profit and Non-Profit Organizations. *Management Science* 36 (4): 436–48.

Sherif, M. 1958. Superordinate Goals in the Reduction of Intergroup Conflict. *The American Journal of Sociology* 63 (4): 349–56.

Slevin, D. P. 1991. *The Whole Manager*. New York: AMACOM.

Slevin, D. P., and J. G. Covin. 1990. Juggling Entrepreneurial Style and Organizational Structure: How to Get Your Act Together. *Sloan Management Review* 31 (2): 123–35.

Slevin, D. P., and J. K. Pinto. 1987. Balancing Strategy and Tactics in Project Implementation. *Sloan Management Review* 29: 33–47.

———. 1988. Leadership, Motivation, and the Project Manager. In *The Project Management Handbook*, 2d ed., edited by D. I. Cleland and W. R. King. New York: Van Nostrand Reinhold, 739–70.

———. 1991. Project Leadership: Understanding and Consciously Choosing Your Style. *Project Management Journal* 22 (1): 39–47.

Souder, W. E. 1988. Managing Relations between R&D and Marketing in New Product Development Projects. *Journal of Product Innovation Management* 5: 6–19.

Spirer, H. F., and D. H. Hamburger. 1988. Phasing Out the Project. In *Project Management Handbook*, edited by D. I. Cleland and W. R. King. New York: Van Nostrand Reinhold, 231–50.

Srinivasan, A., and J. G. Davis. 1987. A Reassessment of Implementation Process Models. *Interfaces* 17 (3): 64–71.

Stogdill, R. 1984. *Handbook of Leadership*. New York: Free Press.

Stuckenbruck, L. C. 1978. Project Manager—The Systems Integrator. *Project Management Quarterly* 9 (4): 31–38.

Takeuchi, H., and I. Nonaka. 1986. The New Product Development Game. *Harvard Business Review* 64 (1): 137–46.

Tjosvold, D. 1984. Effects of Leader Warmth and Directiveness on Subordinate Performance on a Subsequent Task. *Journal of Applied Psychology* 69: 422–27.

Tuchman, B. W., and M. A. Jensen. 1977. Stages in Small Group Development Revisited. *Group and Organizational Studies* 2: 419–27.

Valacich, Joseph S., and Charles Schwenk. 1995. Structuring Conflict in Individual, Face-to-Face, and Computer-Mediated Group Decision-Making: Carping versus Objective Devil's Advocacy. *Decision Sciences Journal* 26 (3): 369–93.

Vanlommel, E., and B. DeBrabander. 1975. The Organization of Electronic Data Processing (EDP) Activities and Computer Use. *Journal of Business* 48: 391–410.

Vroom, V. H. and P. W. Yetton. 1973. *Leadership and Decision Making.* Pittsburgh, PA: University of Pittsburgh Press.

Wellar, B. 1988. Institutional Maxims and Conditions for Needs-Sensitive Information Systems and Services in Local Governments. *Proceedings of the Urban and Regional Information Systems Association*, vol. 4. Washington, DC: Urban and Regional Information Systems Association, 371–78.

Recommended Reading

Badiru, A. B. 1996. *Project Management in Manufacturing and High Technology Operations*, 2d ed. New York: Wiley.

Gido, J., and J. P. Clements. 1999. *Successful Project Management*. Cincinnati, OH: Southwestern.

Meredith, J., and S. Mantel Jr. 1995. *Project Management*, 3d ed. New York: Wiley.

Pinto, J. K., and J. G. Covin. 1989. Critical Factors in Project Implementation: A Comparison of Construction and R&D Projects. *Technovation* 9: 49–62.

> This study explores the differences in critical-factor importance across two broad categories of projects: construction and R&D. It reports on the findings of a study that suggests that these critical factors vary not only at different stages of the project life cycle, but also from one major type of project to another.

Pinto, J. K., and J. E. Prescott. 1988. Variations in Critical Success Factors Over the Stages in the Project Life Cycle. *Journal of Management* 14: 5–18.

> The importance of this research is that it demonstrates that critical success factors for projects vary in importance across different stages in the project life cycle. The findings offer important implications for managing these key points more effectively.

Additional Research on Critical Success Factors

Pinto, J. K., and J. G. Covin. 1989. Critical Factors in Project Implementation: A Comparison of Construction and R&D Projects. *Technovation* 9: 49–62.

> This study explores the differences in critical-factor importance across two broad categories of projects: construction and R&D. It reports on the findings of a study that suggests that these critical factors vary, not only at different stages of the project life cycle, but also from one major type of project to another.

Pinto, J. K., and J. E. Prescott. 1988. Variations in Critical Success Factors Over the Stages in the Project Life Cycle. *Journal of Management* 14: 5–18.

> The importance of this research was to demonstrate that critical success factors for projects vary in importance across different stages in the project life cycle. The findings offer important implications for managing these key points more effectively.

Pinto, J. K., and D. P. Slevin. 1992. The Project Implementation Profile. Tuxedo, NY: Xicom, Inc.

> Offers a ten-item self-assessment instrument for project managers interested in tracking their projects.

Upgrade Your Project Management Knowledge with First-Class Publications from PMI

Project Management Software Survey

The PMI® *Project Management Software Survey* offers an efficient way to compare and contrast the capabilities of a wide variety of project management tools. More than two hundred software tools are listed with comprehensive information on systems features, how they perform time analysis, resource analysis, cost analysis, performance analysis, and cost reporting, and how they handle multiple projects, project tracking, charting, and much more. The survey is a valuable tool to help narrow the field when selecting the best project management tools.
ISBN: 1-880410-52-4 (paperback), ISBN: 1-880410-59-1 (CD-ROM)

The Juggler's Guide to Managing Multiple Projects

This comprehensive book introduces and explains task-oriented, independent, and interdependent levels of project portfolios. It says that you must first have a strong foundation in time management and priority setting, then introduces the concept of Portfolio Management to timeline multiple projects, determine their resource requirements, and handle emergencies, putting you in charge for possibly the first time in your life!
ISBN: 1-880410-65-6 (paperback)

Recipes for Project Success

This book is destined to become "the" reference book for beginning project managers, particularly those who like to cook! Practical, logically developed project management concepts are offered in easily understood terms in a lighthearted manner. They are applied to the everyday task of cooking—from simple, single dishes, such as homemade tomato sauce for pasta, made from the bottom up, to increasingly complex dishes or meals for groups that in turn require an understanding of more complex project management terms and techniques. The transistion between cooking and project management discussions is smooth, and tidbits of information provided with the receipes are interesting and humorous.
ISBN: 1-880410-58-3 (paperback)

TOOLS AND TIPS FOR TODAY'S PROJECT MANAGER

This guide book is valuable for understanding project management and performing to quality standards. Includes project management concepts and terms—old and new—that are not only defined but also are explained in much greater detail than you would find in a typical glossary. Also included are tips on handling such seemingly simple everyday tasks as how to say "No" and how to avoid telephone tag. It's a reference you'll want to keep close at hand.
ISBN: 1-880410-61-3 (paperback)

THE FUTURE OF PROJECT MANAGEMENT

The project management profession is going through tremendous change—both evolutionary and revolutionary. Some of these changes are internally driven while many are externally driven. Here, for the first time, is a composite view of some major trends occurring throughout the world and the implication of them on the profession of project management and on the Project Management Institute. Read the views of the 1998 PMI Research Program Team, a well-respected futurist firm, and other authors. This book represents the beginning of a journey and, through inputs from readers and others, it will continue as a work in progress.
ISBN: 1-880410-71-0 (paperback)

NEW RESOURCES FOR PMP CANDIDATES

The following publications are resources that certification candidates can use to gain information on project management theory, principles, techniques, and procedures.

PMP RESOURCE PACKAGE

Earned Value Project Management
    by Quentin W. Fleming and Joel M. Koppelman

Effective Project Management: How to Plan, Manage, and Deliver Projects on Time and Within Budget
    by Robert K. Wysocki, et al.

A Guide to the Project Management Body of Knowledge (PMBOK™ Guide)
    by the PMI Standards Committee

Human Resource Skills for the Project Manager
    by Vijay K. Verma

The New Project Management
    by J. Davidson Frame

Organizing Projects for Success
    by Vijay K. Verma

Principles of Project Management
    by John Adams, et al.

Project & Program Risk Management
    by R. Max Wideman, Editor

Project Management Casebook
    edited by David I. Cleland, et al.

Project Management: A Managerial Approach, Third Edition
    by Jack R. Meredith and Samuel J. Mantel, Jr.

Project Management: A Systems Approach to Planning, Scheduling, and Controlling, Sixth Edition
    by Harold Kerzner

A GUIDE TO THE PROJECT MANAGEMENT BODY OF KNOWLEDGE (PMBOK™ GUIDE)

The basic management reference for everyone who works on projects. Serves as a tool for learning about the generally accepted knowledge and practices of the profession. As "management by projects" becomes more and more a recommended business practice worldwide, the *PMBOK™ Guide* becomes an essential source of information that should be on every manager's bookshelf. Available in hardcover or paperback, the *PMBOK™ Guide* is an official standards document of the Project Management Institute.
ISBN: 1-880410-12-5 (paperback), ISBN: 1-880410-13-3 (hardcover)

INTERACTIVE PMBOK™ GUIDE

This CD-ROM makes it easy for you to access the valuable information in PMI's *PMBOK™ Guide*. Features hypertext links for easy reference—simply click on underlined words in the text, and the software will take you to that particular section in the *PMBOK™ Guide*. Minimum system requirements: 486 PC; 8MB RAM; 10MB free disk space; CD-ROM drive, mouse, or other pointing device; and Windows 3.1 or greater.

MANAGING PROJECTS STEP-BY-STEP™

Follow the steps, standards, and procedures used and proven by thousands of professional project managers and leading corporations. This interactive multimedia CD-ROM based on PMI's *PMBOK™ Guide* will enable you to customize, standardize, and distribute your project plan standards, procedures, and methodology across your entire organization. Multimedia illustrations using 3-D animations and audio make this perfect for both self-paced training or for use by a facilitator.

PMBOK™ Q&A

Use this handy pocket-sized question-and-answer study guide to learn more about the key themes and concepts presented in PMI's international standard, *PMBOK™ Guide*. More than 160 multiple-choice questions with answers (referenced to the *PMBOK™ Guide*) help you with the breadth of knowledge needed to understand key project management concepts.
ISBN: 1-880410-21-4 (paperback)

PMI PROCEEDINGS LIBRARY CD-ROM

This interactive guide to PMI's annual Seminars & Symposium proceedings offers a powerful new option to the traditional methods of document storage and retrieval, research, training, and technical writing. Contains complete paper presentations from PMI '92–PMI '97 with full-text search capability, convenient onscreen readability, and PC/Mac compatibility.

PMI Publications Library CD-ROM

Using state-of-the-art technology, PMI offers complete articles and information from its major publications on one CD-ROM, including *PM Network* (1990–97), *Project Management Journal* (1990–97), and *A Guide to the Project Management Body of Knowledge*. Offers full-text search capability and indexing by *PMBOK*™ *Guide* knowledge areas. Electronic indexing schemes and sophisticated search engines help to find and retrieve articles quickly that are relevant to your topic or research area.

Also Available from PMI

Project Management for Managers
Mihály Görög, Nigel J. Smith
ISBN: 1-880410-54-0 (paperback)

Project Leadership: From Theory to Practice
Jeffery K. Pinto, Peg Thoms, Jeffrey Trailer, Todd Palmer, Michele Govekar
ISBN: 1-880410-10-9 (paperback)

Annotated Bibliography of Project and Team Management
David I. Cleland, Gary Rafe, Jeffrey Mosher
ISBN: 1-880410-47-8 (paperback),
ISBN: 1-880410-57-5 (CD-ROM)

How to Turn Computer Problems into Competitive Advantage
Tom Ingram
ISBN: 1-880410-08-7 (paperback)

Achieving the Promise of Information Technology
Ralph B. Sackman
ISBN: 1-880410-03-6 (paperback)

Leadership Skills for Project Managers
Editors' Choice Series
Edited by Jeffrey K. Pinto, Jeffrey W. Trailer
ISBN: 1-880410-49-4 (paperback)

The Virtual Edge
Margery Mayer
ISBN: 1-880410-16-8 (paperback)

ABCs of DPC
Edited by PMI's Design-Procurement-Construction Specific Interest Group
ISBN: 1-880410-07-9 (paperback)

Project Management Casebook
Edited by David I. Cleland, Karen M. Bursic, Richard Puerzer, A. Yaroslav Vlasak
ISBN: 1-880410-45-1 (paperback)

Project Management Casebook Instructor's Manual
Edited by David I. Cleland, Karen M. Bursic, Richard Puerzer, A. Yaroslav Vlasak
ISBN: 1-880410-18-4 (paperback)

PMI Book of Project Management Forms
ISBN: 1-880410-31-1 (paperback)
ISBN: 1-880410-50-8 (diskette version 1.0)

Principles of Project Management
John Adams et al.
ISBN: 1-880410-30-3 (paperback)

Organizing Projects for Success
Human Aspects of Project Management Series, Volume 1, Vijay K. Verma
ISBN: 1-880410-40-0 (paperback)

Human Resource Skills for the Project Manager
Human Aspects of Project Management Series, Volume 2, Vijay K. Verma
ISBN: 1-880410-41-9 (paperback)

ORDER ONLINE AT
WWW.PMIBOOKSTORE.ORG

Book Ordering Information

Phone: 412.741.6206

Fax: 412.741.0609

Email: pmiorders@abdintl.com

Mail: PMI Publications Fulfillment Center,
PO Box 1020,
Sewickley, Pennsylvania 15143-1020 USA